HOOK
ON A
GOOD THING

HOOKED
ON A
GOOD THING

SAMMY HALL
with Charles Paul Conn

P.O. Box 4777
Sevierville, TN 37864
(865) 453-8579

Library of Congress Cataloging in Publication Data

Hall, Sammy.
    Hooked on a good thing.

    1. Conversion.   I. Conn, Charles Paul, joint author.   II. Title.
BV4935.H24A3   248'.4   72-3826
ISBN 0-8007-0548-3

CHAPTER 1

"Isn't he the sweetest little thing you ever did see? That skinny little body and that big, wide open mouth! I declare, I've never seen the like in my life—the way he stands up there on that altar bench and rears back his head and sings! He's just about the sweetest little thing I ever *did* see!"

That was me they were talking about.

Skinny, but sweet. And loud. That was the way they always described me back in those days, those hard-working women in their cotton print dresses and work-calloused hands and hair all tied up in neat, stern buns on the backs of their heads. They were the backbone of that little Pentecostal church in Sanford, North Carolina, where I was a boy, and they were my very first audience.

I was three years old at the time, and I remember them well. I don't remember being skinny and I don't remember being sweet, but you'd better believe I remember standing on that altar bench and rearing back my head and singing.

My dad was the accompanist in those days, strumming an old beat-up guitar, picking a note or two here and there, always poker-faced and serious. And I'd take those church songs he taught me so carefully back home and fling them at the congregation with all the volume I could muster. Face flushed, jugular vein jumping, I cranked out the music to those familiar, smiling faces, and I loved every minute of it.

Soon my family moved to Fort Lauderdale, Florida, but only the geography changed. The setting inside the church was virtually the same: still a small, loyal congregation of the faithful willing to listen to a skinny mountain boy sing from atop a shaky altar bench.

Singing and churchgoing. They made a natural pair then, with Dad emphasizing the singing and my mom mostly interested in the churchgoing. As for me, it was many years before I learned that one was even possible without the other.

Mom was not the kind of woman who would particularly stand out from the crowd in a small southern church. Her hair was grey with streaks of white; her dresses she wore well below the knee, and her tendency to freckle was a trait which she passed on to me in abundance.

Ever since I can remember, Mom has known God in that direct, no nonsense way that made our home a thoroughly Christian one, and all of us in it churchgoers whether we liked it or not.

Dad taught me to play the guitar, and I always suspected that he enjoyed strumming along while I sang more than he enjoyed anything else about church in those days. He never said much about spiritual things, but early in the game he wrapped me so tightly around his heart that, years later, when he finally spoke, I listened.

We shared lots of things that are common to fathers and sons, but most of all we shared a love for music. After he taught me to whang around on his old guitar, he decided I was old enough for one of my own. When he bought it for me, the world was too small to contain us! Onto the school bus I climbed, dragging that secondhand guitar behind. I scarcely knew the meaning of the word *hick*, and I daily drowned the smirks of my Florida classmates in a flood of Marty Robbins, Webb Pierce, and Hank Williams. Whether they liked it or not!

I thought, *"Grand Ole Opry," here I come!* But the little church we attended provided a more accessible audience, and there it was that I sang and whanged and whetted my appetite for the stage.

There was always a supporting cast. Two sisters, Bernice and Vonceil, were older than me by five and four years. Jimmy was three years older, and a third sister, Judy, trailed me in the family pecking order by three years. All were musical, and all took turns trying out childhood talents on the church.

I loved to sing, and my memories of those very early, very innocent days are warm and pleasant. But the older I got, the less I enjoyed the simple pleasures of church, and the more eagerly I sought ways to avoid it.

Mom had a simple rule for church attendance: unless you were dead or dying, you went to church every time the doors were open. Sunday school became a bore and a burden. By the time I was eleven, I had come to resent so hotly being made to go to church that I stopped singing solos in the worship services. I was determined not to enjoy *anything* about church, so I refused to sing when they asked. Sorry, sore throat. Sorry, laryngitis. Sorry, bad cold. So finally they got the point or ran out of patience or something, because finally they didn't bother to ask anymore.

Sunday became the dreariest day of the week for me. I was determined to hate it, and hate it I did. I fidgeted. I squirmed. I played sick. I played hooky. I drove my Sunday-school teacher to distraction. And when I could get away with it, I sneaked out of the building, went down to the grocery store on the corner, and ate crackers and drank Cokes until the service dismissed.

What impressed me most about church was the preaching, and what impressed me most about the preaching was the preaching about hell. Nothing grabbed my attention quite like a sermon, fervently and passionately delivered, which described hell in all its fiery detail. I listened. I listened because I was afraid not to, and many was the time that I sat on the edge of my pew in petrified attention until the subject of hell was exhausted. When that subject was finished, so was my interest in the sermon.

Though my rebellion against the church was already beginning, there was never a time as a child when I did not believe what I was hearing in those sermons. I knew that God was real; I saw His power demonstrated time and time again. Often I had a keen sense of guilt and judgment, and the harder the preachers preached, the worse I felt.

I heard many sermons on the Second Coming then, and more than once I had those hairy-scary dreams that the Lord had returned for the rapture of the church and I had been left.

And so I learned to pray. I learned to pray until I felt better, pray until I wasn't scared anymore. I didn't really pray to God, I don't think, as much as I prayed just to be talking to myself, trying to go through some kind of little ritual in hopes that perhaps that would forestall impending judgment. I remember praying, "God, I know I'm a sinner, but please don't let me die without a chance to make things right with you."

I made many trips to the altar as a child and a young teen-ager, but never did I make a commitment of my life to God. They were emotional trips sometimes, prompted by fear and accompanied by short-lived tears. They were social trips sometimes, made to avoid being the oddball when everyone else was going down the aisle.

But somehow I never even came close to becoming a disciple of Jesus Christ. I never even seriously considered turning my life over to Him. It was now-I-lay-me-down-to-sleep when I was worried about judgment, and no thought of God at all when I wasn't.

Altar services were long and serious at our little Church of God in Fort Lauderdale, and I usually ducked out as early as possible. That became the pattern: suffer through the sermon, bow my head solemnly until the congregation had filled the altar, then slip outside to stand around and goof off with the other teen-age boys.

On one such night I was clowning around in the darkness outside the church, oblivious to the prayers of the saints who were plainly visible through the open windows. I was playing for laughs that night, and I started to run madly across the church lawn, imitating one of the worshipers inside.

It was great fun until I hit that tree. Oh, how I hit that tree! I ran smack into it, running hard in the darkness, and it didn't budge an inch. I either sprawled, crumpled, lurched, or flopped to the ground—I'll never know which, because I was out cold as a mackerel.

My buddies carried me inside the church and laid me, still unconscious, on the front pew. They were scared. The pastor called the congregation around me and they prayed fervently for me as I came woozily back to my senses. My head hurt too badly and my stomach felt too weak to do anything but mutter a humble "thank you" and stumble on rubbery legs toward the door and home. Sometimes a good sturdy tree can teach a fellow more respect for God's house in two seconds than a whole churchful of Sunday-school teachers can teach him in a lifetime.

For every rule imposed by the church and my parents during that time, I found five ways to break it. And whom do you suppose I sought out for companionship in my mischief? The preacher's kid, of course.

I remember the pastor as being a good one during my early teen years. He was genuinely interested in the youth of the church, and made every effort to reach us. But I just wasn't interested, and neither was his son, Ronnie, and together we thought of ourselves as something like the Junior High Mafia of the local church.

Among the forbidden pastimes was card-playing, so naturally we chose the parsonage as the scene of our first poker game. We sat draped around the dining room table, slouching with such self-conscious carelessness, reveling in our corruption, as we flipped cards back and forth across the table and exchanged our most degenerate-looking sneers.

A car pulled up outside and out stepped Ron's dad. Pastor Shoemaker, in the flesh. We jumped to our feet, frantically began scraping together all the cards from off the table and floor, and barely won the race, Ron sticking the last card into my hand just as the pastor put his hand on the doorknob.

It was then that I panicked. The sudden prospect of that austere minister stepping through the door to find me with a deck of cards in my hand, in *his* house, destroyed whatever presence of mind I had.

I blew my cool, as they say.

So instead of slipping the cards into my pocket or holding them behind my back or sitting on them or something sensible like that, I impulsively heaved the whole deck wildly under the table. Not a bad idea, except that the tablecloth came only halfway to the floor, and the Reverend stepped into the room to the sight of hearts and spades and diamonds and kings and jacks and aces fluttering to the floor in wild profusion at our feet. It was a mistake which we paid for with our hides. Literally.

One night we slipped out of church and climbed atop the parsonage with a big bag of carpet tacks. Somehow, in the dark, unknowable stupidity of the thirteen-year-old mind, it seemed to us that throwing tacks onto the busy highway below would be great fun, an exciting way to spend an otherwise dull and ordinary Sunday evening. Just fun-loving all-American boys we were, and that time, as many times, our peculiar idea of fun was cut rudely short by our parents' old-fashioned idea of punishment.

There was one aspect of church life that I never got soured on, and that was the summer camping program. Our church sponsored a week-long camp for young teens each summer at a place called Wimauma in central Florida, and I always eagerly packed up to go to camp with the kids from the church.

There, away from my family, away from the local setting, my antagonism for religious things seemed always to melt temporarily away, and there at Wimauma I thought more seriously about my need for God than at any other time as a teen-ager. Maybe the weeks were just too short; maybe I just wasn't ready to surrender to God; but somehow I let the time slip away without making a real commitment. Back home again, I always slipped back into the old rut of mindless, reckless rebellion.

As I grew older, the mischief of childhood gave way to more serious problems as a young teen-ager. As I moved up through the grades at Sunrise Junior High School, the influence of church and home faded to zero, and I became more and more involved with undesirable friends at school.

Fads are common among kids of that age, and I wallowed in every one of them from the Yo-Yo to the hula-hoop. But when I was in the ninth grade, a fad hit my group of buddies that was a bit different: shoplifting.

Shoplifting became the thing to do. The number of items you could swipe became the biggest status symbol in my circle of friends, and soon I joined in along with the rest.

I'll never forget the first time I stole something. Next to the school there was a drugstore where we waited for the bus to come each afternoon. I didn't believe that stealing could be as easy as the guys told me, so I went into the store with one of them to watch him steal a ball-point pen. Into the store, pick up the pen, out of the store. No sweat.

So then it was my turn. I was scared, but grimly determined not to choke out in front of my buddies. I went back into the drugstore, back to the same counter of pens, saw that I was unwatched, and decided to go my buddy one better. I grabbed a whole handful of pens, ten or twelve at least, crammed them into my shirt, and headed for the door with my heart doing double time.

Safely out on the sidewalk, I handed out the pens to the admiring audience with many a grand gesture and loud bravado, and from then on I began to think of myself as some kind of superthief, king of the ninth-grade shoplifters.

That drugstore became a daily target. As we waited for the bus each day, we took turns going in to steal, daring one another to go for loot again and again. We almost cleaned the druggist out before one of the guys got caught, and we quit there and went on to try our luck somewhere else.

I thought it was really a big deal to swipe something, and I loved the attention I got from the other guys for my exploits. I would bet them that I could steal a certain amount of merchandise, and I wouldn't come out of the store until I had it.

I got hooked. I really got hooked on shoplifting. It became a passion with me, a compulsion, almost a sickness. I stole things I didn't want, didn't need, didn't know why I was taking. Long before I started smoking with any frequency, I stole cartons of cigarettes by the dozens and threw them away or hid them around the neighborhood.

Once I saw the manager of a store eye me from across the aisle, then whisper something to a clerk, who whispered something to the cashier. I went up an aisle hidden from view, dumped the stuff I had swiped onto a counter, then headed for the door. The cashier grabbed me with a look of triumph, summoned the manager, and together they searched me and found . . . nothing.

Eventually shoplifting wasn't even fun anymore. I did it because I had to. I did it when I didn't want to. I pushed myself to go for bigger and bigger items. I would keep the stuff, sell it if I could, throw it away, give it to people, anything. The thrill was gone and only the compulsion remained.

Finally I got caught, and only then was I able to quit. Ironically, it was a five-and-ten store, and I was stealing a notebook. The manager chewed me out and let me go, and after that my thieving dwindled to nothing. I was lucky. When I think of what could have happened, I still want to kick myself for my ninth-grade stupidity.

In only one area of my life did I do anything constructive during junior high school. That was in music.

My parents had been very strict, and generally discouraged me from participation in activities outside the church and home. My sisters and I couldn't attend the high-school football games, or wear gym shorts during physical education, so we just didn't get involved in many things. Music was different. Apart from my early lessons from Dad, my folks encouraged me to learn all the music I could, and to get involved in all the musical activity I could.

Dad owned a little produce market on Oakland Park Boulevard, and one of his regular customers was an old Italian gentleman named Anthony Caruso. Mr. Caruso was a music teacher, and one day when I was eight, he stopped by the produce market and Dad asked me to sing for him. I did; he liked me; and a long, happy friendship began that day.

Mr. Caruso taught voice and guitar. For me there could have been no more fortunate combination. He took me under his wing, gave me free lessons, made me practice, made me work. He taught me more guitar licks in the first lesson than I ever knew existed. Throughout grammar school and junior high, he worked with me and brought me along musically.

I never understood what the payoff was for Mr. Caruso, never knew what he was getting out of our relationship. Nothing, I guess, except a genuine pleasure in giving to someone else and watching him grow. And that he did. He worked with me until I was sixteen years old, then gave me an old '52 Ford for about half what the car was worth, and cut me loose from his musical apron strings.

Except for the musical progress I made, I guess you

would have to say that my junior-high years were an un-
qualified flop. What should have been the most important
thing going, my relationship with God, was nowhere. I
was soured on the church. My attitude toward my family
was belligerent. My behavior was becoming recklessly
irresponsible.

And things were going to get worse.

CHAPTER 2

I NEVER INTENDED to become a teen-age beer bum.

Believe me, when I entered Fort Lauderdale High School as a sophomore, the prospect of ever becoming a heavy drinker was the farthest thing from my mind. I was sixteen years old and ready to take the place by storm, ready to become a Big Man On Campus in record time.

It never happened. I hear lots of people tell about their high-school days and list all their accomplishments and awards, elections to this and that, and I just have to sit back and envy their achievements. None of those nice things ever happened to me. I made worse than average grades, never held any student office, never was any kind of high-school leader. I hit Fort Lauderdale High with all kinds of dreams and ambitions, and left there a year and a half later without accomplishing a thing. I was a dud.

There was a reason, and the reason was alcohol.

I took my first drink at the age of thirteen, and at

the time it didn't seem like such a big deal. I had some cousins who lived in Fort Myers, over on Florida's Gulf Coast, and I visited them often during the summer months.

I was the youngest kid in the group during those visits, and I enjoyed hanging around with the older guys. One day things were dull and slow and we were all sitting around in the sweltering Saturday afternoon heat, trying to think of someway to beat back the boredom.

"Sammy."

"Yeah."

"Hey, Sammy."

"Yeah."

"I bet you don't know what it's like to get drunk, do you?"

"I might and I might not."

He smelled the scent of innocence, and spoke now more loudly, with a bit more animation, and the guys began to stir. "Come on, Sammy, I bet you've never even had a beer before, have you?"

Silence. I could feel them looking at me.

"Have you?" It was an accusation more than a question this time, and it demanded an answer.

"Nope, I don't reckon I have."

"Let's go, fellows, we're going to have a little fun!" So up we jumped and off we trooped toward the friendly neighborhood package store, them to relieve the tedium of a hot summer day, me to taste the devil's brew for the first time ever.

We got a couple of six-packs, and drove around Fort

Myers drinking and congratulating ourselves on our great daring and manliness. I sipped while they guzzled. They asked me how I liked it. I said okay. We drove some more and drank some more. I felt a little woozy and a little sick. They asked me how I liked it. This time I said great, though I felt no different from the time before, and that seemed to please them more.

I didn't drink very much that day—maybe a can and a half, maybe two cans of beer—but it was an experience that had an enormous impact on me and my future. I had broken an important barrier, and it marked the beginning of a whole new world for me. It was as if I had crossed an invisible line, and now there was no turning back.

Life has always been like that for me, and for lots of other people too, I suppose. Once a thing is done for the first time, the barrier is down and there is little reason to hold back. Until I took my first drink, I thought of drinking as something I didn't do, and I was never tempted by it. Somehow, with that first can of beer, all of that changed. I now suddenly accepted drinking as a part of my behavior, and never again did I consider it a thing that I could not and would not do. It just didn't seem wrong anymore.

When I started high school, the occasional visits to the package store became more and more frequent, and early in the tenth grade I got really drunk for the first time. One Friday a friend of mine whispered to me at school that his folks were going away for the weekend, and suggested that we take advantage of the chance to booze it up at his house.

The next afternoon the two of us sat down at the

kitchen table with a stack of unopened beer cans and a determination to get as drunk as possible as soon as possible. We succeeded grandly, and compared hangovers with each other the next day like they were our own special badges of accomplishment.

That was the first of many such weekends. Beer soon began to seem a bit juvenile, and I went to harder stuff, bourbon, whiskey, vodka. At first I used the harder liquor to spike the beer, then learned to drink it straight, and in larger and larger quantities.

By the end of that sophomore year, I was drinking heavily almost every weekend. I became preoccupied with the whole scene: getting the booze, slipping off somewhere with a few buddies, and getting smashed right out of my head.

I lost interest in everything else. I didn't study. I didn't date. I quit practicing my guitar. I became a weekend drunk, and the only thing that I and my little circle of friends thought about was getting stoned on the weekends. That's what we always talked about at school—rehashing our drinking experiences of the weekend before or laying plans for the weekend ahead.

Looking back, I ask the question "Why?" and there is no sensible answer. It cost me a lot. Since I hid my drinking from my parents, my relationship with them became strained and unpleasant. To keep them in the dark, I had to live a double life, lying to them virtually every day, going to ridiculous extremes to keep them from knowing what I was into.

Drinking also cost me all of the hopes that I had for

myself in high school. It made me a loser, a misfit, one of those guys who slinks around the school in his own little private world, enjoying little and learning nothing.

Why? I don't know—I just got hooked, that's why. I got to where I didn't drink for fun; I drank to get drunk. I got to where I drank by myself, and the worse I felt about it, the more I drank. It was just like the shoplifting, the same old trap, ruining myself without the slightest idea why.

I had one friend during my high-school and junior-high-school years who was as close as any friend I've ever had. I'll call him Freddy Turner, though that's not his real name. Freddy and I practically grew up together in Fort Lauderdale, went to the same schools from grade school up. We spent virtually all our time together as teen-agers, laid out of school together, got into mischief together; and I was closer to him than to my own brother.

Freddy was dark-skinned, of Spanish extraction. He was short and very muscular, with dark hair and even white teeth that always showed when he smiled, which was most of the time. He spent lots of time at my house, occasionally worked with my dad at the produce market, and was a favorite with both my parents.

Freddy was a year older than I was, but drinking was something that I introduced to him. When I came back from Fort Myers that summer, I told him about the episode with the beer, and he agreed to try it. It was the last time I ever had to encourage him to drink, because from then on, as in most things, he took the lead.

We became beer bums together, and we knew we were drinking too much, Freddy and I. We supported one another, urged one another on. He had quite a reputation for being able to drink a lot, and took great pride in the large amounts of booze he could consume. He laid me in the shade on that score, and in the end his reputation for being able to "put away the juice" killed him.

Early in my junior year, a buddy of ours came home on leave from the Navy, and Freddy decided to throw a party for him. Freddy's parents had gone up to Riviera Beach for the weekend, and he invited about ten guys over for a Saturday-night drinking party, promising the run of the house and all the hard liquor we could drink.

A few days before the party, Freddy and I had a big fight. It was a silly argument over a girl whom he had dated. He thought I had insulted her or something—I can't even remember now what it was all about. The important thing was that we had quarreled and we were both provoked with each other, so I decided not to go to his party.

I was miserable that night. I drove around by myself for awhile in my old '52 Ford, stopped in at a drive-in movie for a few minutes, finally went home and went to bed. Early the next morning I decided to quit being so stubborn and go on over to Freddy's house. I got up while it was still dark, dressed, and headed that way.

I drove down the block toward Freddy's house with the sun just coming up, eager to get with the guys and end my self-imposed solitude. It was about 7:00 A.M., and as I swung into the driveway I saw the red and white ambulance backed up to the door of the house. My heart almost stopped beating.

The door swung open and out burst Jack, tears crawling down his cheeks. He grabbed me by both arms, and with a whining, high-pitched sob, told me the news.

"He's dead. He's dead."

The voice was other-worldly, almost unreal, and the silence that followed it was heavy and painful and full of tragedy.

"What are you talking about? Who's dead?" I asked the question without wanting to hear the answer because somehow I knew the answer already. Freddy was dead. Stone-cold dead. And there was nothing anybody could do about it.

Before Jack could reply, the ambulance attendants came pushing through the back door of the house, pulling behind them a stretcher on which Freddy lay, the sheet already tucked carefully around his face, so that all I could see was his form under the sheet. And behind the stretcher filed a long, sad line of pale, angular faces, red-eyed from the night's revelry, skin blanched white and sober by the sudden tragedy.

"Freddy's dead." Jack said it then, and when he had gotten the words out once, he said it over and over, to himself and to me and to whomever was hearing. "Freddy's dead. Freddy's dead." And he said it long after the ambulance had pulled out to leave us, stunned, paralyzed, standing on the gravel driveway, trying to absorb it. "Freddy's dead. Freddy's dead."

In the time before the funeral on Tuesday, the story was told over and over. The party had been a roaring success, and Freddy had boasted that he could outdrink anyone there. He bet one of the guys that he could drink two fifths of whiskey, straight, without stopping. Impossible, they said. No one can drink that much whiskey, they said. It would kill a guy, they said.

But Freddy was as good as his boast, and down the whiskey went. In one big, long chug-a-lug. Two fifths. And then Freddy passed out on the floor. They thought he would sleep it off, but when he didn't wake up in a couple of hours, they put him in a tub of cold water, then turned the cold shower on him, but couldn't revive him. So they put him to bed.

At about 6:00 A.M., Freddy started to breathe rapidly in hard, loud breaths, and the boys, now thoroughly frightened, decided they should call the hospital. While the ambulance was on its way, Freddy died in the bed, with all his buddies huddled weakly around.

I will never forget the nightmare of those days after his death. I will never forget my feeling of guilt, and fear, and sickness. I kept a constant vigil at the funeral home, and that face in the coffin has haunted me ever since. For months it glowed before me at night. I couldn't get it out of my mind.

They buried Freddy on Tuesday, and on Tuesday night, I made a solemn promise to God. "God," I said, "I'll never drink another drop of liquor as long as I live." I was frightened and sick at heart. "I swear to you, God," I promised that night, "I swear to you I'll never drink again. Never. For any reason. I promise you that, God."

The weeks that followed Freddy's death seemed empty and eventless, and for a while I kept my promise to God that I would never drink again. Maybe, I thought, this thing has happened to get me sobered up and straightened out. Maybe this is what it took to get me to change.

One day without warning I went back to the sauce. I was talking to a fellow at work one day, a man whom I hardly even knew. I told him that I didn't drink because I thought it was wrong, and because I thought it was dangerous and damaging. He laughed at the arguments and, one at a time, shot them down.

It is silly and old-fashioned not to drink, he said. It is a shame to miss out on the good life just because a friend dies, he said. It is relaxing and enjoyable to drink, he said. It is foolish and childish to believe in God, he said.

Stupidly, I believed him. I remember thinking how logical all his arguments seemed. What good sense they made. So, just like that, I began to drink again. I dismissed my promises to God, told myself that they were made under the stress of Freddy's death, and that I didn't need to keep those promises.

Within weeks I was drinking hard and heavy again, as frustrated and miserable as ever. But with Freddy gone, it was never quite the same at Fort Lauderdale High School for me, and life became a long, tiresome, unhappy routine. All over again, just like before, I was in a trap of my own weakness, and it was eating at me.

Then I hit upon the answer! What I needed was a change—a change of scenery, friends, atmosphere, everything. I needed to leave Fort Lauderdale, leave its bad memories and influences, and go somewhere to get a fresh start, a place where I could really find myself and get my life squared away with God.

A few years earlier, my sisters had attended a small church college near Chattanooga, Tennessee, and had come home enthusiastic about its rich Christian atmosphere. The college had an academy division, serving the three grades of senior high school, and from the moment I first thought of it, this seemed the answer to my dilemma.

I had several hundred dollars saved at that time from a part-time job, and I decided to use it to go to school in Tennessee. It seemed a perfect opportunity. I talked it over with my parents, and they were ecstatic.

So it was settled. I would withdraw from Fort Lauderdale High at the end of the January term and enroll at the Christian academy in Tennessee. There I could get away from my old environment and find the courage and the determination to start a new life. Surely if I could do it anywhere, I could do it there.

So off I went in the last week of January, a high-school junior, off to attend school eight hundred miles from home, off to start a new life far away from all my old problems.

CHAPTER 3

MY SISTERS WERE RIGHT. It *was* a school with a rich Christian atmosphere; and as soon as I arrived there, I knew that this was going to be my best chance to leave my past behind me.

The campus was in the small East Tennessee town of Cleveland, not far from the mountains. There were lots of rules, and certain punishment for breaking them, but I was accustomed to that, and enrolled the day after arriving on campus with spirits high.

On Sunday nights there were chapel services, and all students were required to attend. The President was Dr. Ray H. Hughes, and he preached in chapel on the first Sunday night I was there. He preached powerfully and persuasively, and I sank lower and lower into my seat as time for the altar invitation approached. I ought to go down there, I thought. I ought to go down to that altar and give my heart to God and really get started off right. But I held back. Maybe later, I thought. Maybe after I get

29

acquainted around here. Maybe then I'll become a Christian. But not right now.

I was assigned to an old dormitory called Ellis Hall. The dorm supervisor was a young guy named Echols, and the favorite sport on the hall was keeping him awake at night. All the other fellows there were academy students like myself, and it didn't take long to get acquainted and settle into the campus routine.

I got off to a good start. I was going to class, studying, finding time occasionally to practice my guitar in the Music Building next door, and generally feeling very good about myself. Except on Sunday nights. On Sunday nights came the chapel services, when President Hughes preached and the Holy Spirit moved and I stubbornly held out against God. I was making it fine by myself, I figured, so I didn't need God to straighten out my life anymore. That's what I told myself, but still I felt guilty and restless during those Sunday-night chapel services.

I had been on campus for about six weeks when the bottom dropped out.

It all began late one night when a bunch of us were sitting around the Ellis Hall TV room watching the Ed Sullivan Show. The Beatles were the hottest thing in show business then, and were making their dramatic first tour of the United States. This was the early sixties, when the English rock quartet was at its peak of popularity, and as I watched them play and sing that night, I had a sudden, surging homesickness for the old life, the old sounds, the old atmosphere.

Rock music had been in my blood from my earliest teen

years in Fort Lauderdale, and now as I watched the tiny images of the Beatles on the TV screen, I missed the whole rock scene terribly. It occurred to me that I hadn't heard a live rock group perform in almost two months, since coming to Cleveland. By the time the Beatles shook hands with Ed Sullivan and ran offstage to the screams of the young, rowdy audience, I had decided to find me some good, live, rock music.

The next weekend I got my chance. Mike, another boy on the hall who was a rock fan, told me about a big dance at City High School in Chattanooga that Friday night. A rock band with a big local reputation was playing, and we devised a plan to go hear them. We would say we were going to visit Mike's aunt and uncle in Alabama, get off the bus in Chattanooga, and stay there all weekend.

We signed the right papers, told the right lies, and Friday at dusk we were on the bus rolling toward Chattanooga. Off at the bus station, we headed first to find something to drink, then, feeling a little high, decided to walk to the high school. We couldn't find it. The more we searched, the more lost we were, and the more uneasy we became. It was getting late, and we were in a bad section of town, so finally we stopped on the street to ask an old wino for directions.

"You wanna know where City High School is, do ya?" He looked grubby and boozy as he asked the question. "What are you young fellows doing, just looking for action?"

We didn't answer, so he went right into his sales pitch, scratching his unshaven face as he talked. He knew a beautiful young girl, he said. She was sixteen years old, and a real beauty, he said. And she was ours for four bucks apiece, the bargain of a lifetime, take it or leave it.

We took it. We figured, what the heck, it was getting late, we might never find the stupid dance anyway, and this was just too good to pass up. That's what we told each other as we followed the old bum around the back of an old building and up dark, creaky stairs to a second-floor apartment.

I really didn't want to go, but I assumed that Mike was experienced in such things, and I sure wasn't going to admit to him that I had never been to bed with a woman before, much less like this. No sir. I wasn't going to throw a damper on things for him now. I found out after it was too late that he was thinking the same things about me. It was a first for both of us: we were both scared and didn't know what we were doing; and we both kept up a big, swaggering front to impress each other.

The prostitute that he led us to was not as advertised. She was heavyset and frumpy, at least thirty-five years old, garishly made-up, and the whole experience was disgusting and sick. I was almost nauseated as I waited for Mike to come out of the bedroom, eager to pay and leave.

But the old wino had two easy pigeons in the trap, and he wasn't going to let us get away that easily. As we started to leave, he blocked the door, pulled a pistol from his coat, and took every penny we had between us. Then he slammed the door and we ran. Out of the building, down the stairs, onto the street, and block after block we ran until we were far enough away to feel safe walking again.

Nowhere to go but back to the bus station, where we slept in the waiting room because we had no money now, and no place to go. The next day we tromped all over town, from one hospital to another; we had heard that hospitals would pay for blood donations, and thought that would be an easy way to pick up some quick cash to eat on. No such luck. We were turned away at every clinic we tried, and when Saturday night came we were back on those bus-station benches again, hungry, tired, and frustrated.

The next morning we thumbed back to Cleveland, and were on campus in time for the noon meal. How can I describe how wretched I felt that day? I was sick, tormented by a sense of wrong, knowing that in one reckless night I had blown everything. I hated myself, how bitterly I hated myself for my weakness and my stupidity. Somehow I was sure we would be caught and expelled from school, and all my efforts toward personal reform would be down the drain.

And that's exactly what happened. Our buddies in Ellis Hall knew our plans for the weekend, and were eager to hear how things had gone. We told a couple of them what had happened, and I guess it was just too good a story to keep quiet. By the middle of the week lots of people around campus knew, and on Friday we were summoned to the dean's office.

I had already started packing my stuff when the call came, and by the time the disciplinary action was taken, all my suitcases were stacked in the middle of the dormitory room floor, just waiting for the axe to fall. The presi-

dent called us in, had prayer with us, and officially in-
formed us of our expulsion.

My parents never found out. The phone call that the
president placed to inform them didn't get through, so he
mailed a letter of explanation instead. I called my brother
Jimmy, and he intercepted the letter and tore it up before
it ever got to them. When I arrived back in Fort Lauderdale, I told them I had been dismissed for general disciplinary reasons. They didn't ask for details, and I didn't
volunteer any.

It was then that I gave up on myself. I decided I would
never be able to live right, so I may as well just forget it.
Live it up, have a good time, and plan on going to hell, I
figured. I began to take a fatalistic view of myself, that I
was destined to be a loser. After all, if I couldn't find
myself at a Christian school, where could I?

So I returned home with a heavy, deep, sadness, and I
began immediately to drink more than ever before. I was
a high-school dropout now, with nothing to do, no future
to look forward to. And I felt like I had firmly and fatally
shut the last door between me and God.

Back home, I turned to rock music in earnest. I got a job
as a carpenter's helper, and began to spend all my spare
time hanging around the teen-age discotheques, going to
high-school dances, getting my hand in to play guitar or
sing wherever I could.

It didn't take me long to find out that I was good enough
to hold my own with any of the local rock musicians. I
hadn't done much singing outside of those early days in

church, but as I got more and more into rock music, I found that I could really wail. I began to get lots of chances to fill in with various groups when their vocalists were out for some reason.

My vocal style has always been an unusual combination of country and rock sounds. My earliest influence was country music all the way, hillbilly music and the "Grand Ole Opry" stuff. As I got older, the folk sound came in real big, with groups like the Kingston Trio and Peter, Paul, and Mary, the big names on the national scene.

Folk gave way to rock with the advent of the Beatles, and the soft guitar sounds of folk music yielded to the clanging, hard-driving electric sound. Hard rock came in like a tidal wave, and nothing could have suited me more. Hard rock calls for sheer abandon, for the vocalist to throw himself completely into the music, holding nothing back. In those early days, before a certain amount of so-phistication caught up with it, it was all loud and furious with a big beat that pounded and pounded.

I tore into the hard rock world with a vengeance, and I was *good*. Very good! The first group that I worked with as a regular was called the Impressions, and we did high-school dances and occasional teeny-bopper gigs of various kinds. All of us worked or went to school, of course, and played only in our spare time.

I hadn't been with the Impressions long before I got a chance to jump that group and go with the Mor-Loks, a group in Fort Lauderdale that was a little bigger, a little busier, and a little better known. At the time it was an important step up, and joining the Mor-Loks did wonders for my morale. Things were looking up. We were playing somewhere almost every weekend, and I was doing most of the vocal solos. The money we made wasn't much, but what little we got came so easily that it seemed like more. It didn't matter; I would have worked for nothing, I enjoyed it so much.

It was with the Mor-Loks that I really learned what rock music was all about. I learned how important volume was, how to shout with the microphone almost in my mouth to heighten the impact of the words, how simple body gestures could turn on an eager crowd. I learned the excitement of the pounding, intense beat, and how the kids could be driven almost wild if the beat was strong enough, long enough, loud enough. I learned what it meant to get high on the music itself, so that hours after the gig was over my heart was still too fast and my nerves still too tight to sleep.

I learned how critical the lighting was at a dance, and how much more strongly emotions ran in the semidarkness than when the lights were up. I learned how easy it could be to lose myself, absolutely lose myself, in the music. How I could stand in that spotlight with the mike in my hand and the sound crashing all around me and forget every worry, every problem, forget even who and where I was for those brief, intoxicating moments.

We began to play a few dates outside of Fort Lauderdale, doing mostly high-school dances in neighboring towns in South Florida. The work was not without its hazards. One night in Palm Beach, I walked out to my car after playing at a high-school dance and found about fifty kids from the school milling around the car. Standing by the door was one of the local football players, a real meatball type, hot under the collar because I had made a pass at his girl inside. I was just a skinny little punk and he was going to teach me something about the Palm Beach Chivalry Code right there in front of fifty curious kids.

Before I had a chance to say anything clever, he plastered me in the face with his fist, and grabbed me with the other hand. I can't stand the sight of blood, especially my own. Not being stupid, and not feeling it was the time for bravery, I ran. I had to break loose from him two or three times before I finally struggled into the seat of my car and spun out of the parking lot, but not without a broken windshield, a painfully bruised face, and a badly crumpled ego.

One night in Boca Raton another hostile high-schooler had a similar complaint, but he handled it in a less violent manner. He poured honey into the crankcase of my car engine, and the resulting mess made me a bit more careful about whom I flirted with in the future.

Everything seemed to be going great those days. The only part of my life that was unhappy was my relationship with my parents, and that was coming unglued in a hurry.

My folks were always strict, but before going off to school in Tennessee I was eager for them not to know about my misbehavior. All the rotten things I did, I had to sneak around to do them.

After the episode at the academy, it seemed not to matter anymore. I wasn't in school, and the fact that I was working full time gave me a new feeling of independence from them. So I quit trying to hide my drinking and running around, and told myself that I didn't care what they thought.

The first time I came home drunk was a rude, jarring shock to Mom. It was one thing for her to know that I drank, but somehow quite another for her to see me smashed. I was out late, and didn't expect her to be up when I came in. I thought I could get into the house, go to bed, and sleep it off as usual. I never did find out why she wasn't asleep at that hour.

As I came through the front door, I stumbled clumsily and fell in the middle of the living room floor. I looked up to see her standing over me, her hand over her mouth in a gesture of sudden awareness, as she gasped, "Oh Sammy, you're drunk!" That was all, and she fled to her bedroom. I wobbled into my room and closed the door behind me. Deep into the early hours that night I heard her crying through the thin bedroom walls, sobbing like her heart was shattered, praying for me, begging God to reach me and save me.

I was ashamed that night, genuinely and greviously ashamed, but the feeling just didn't last long enough to make me change. After that first time, I wasn't so careful anymore about the condition in which I came home. Once again, I had crossed a barrier that I had never crossed before, and I got to where I didn't care how Mom saw me.

The bolder I became, the more desperately she worried. The more she worried, the more she talked to me about my need for God. And the more she talked about religion, the more hostile and alienated I grew. It was an ugly, menacing cycle. We were like opposite ends of a magnet, and every time we crossed paths at home there was friction and hard words between us.

I was determined not to let her cram God down my throat. She was determined not to let me be lost in sin. We did nothing but argue, and it was always a Mexican standoff. I came to believe that I truly hated her. She would stand in the living room ironing clothes, or in the kitchen cooking supper, and I would come in from work, shower, change clothes, and start out again. I would brush past her, on my way to play with the Mor-Loks or hear another group or just to drive around and look for some action.

"Son." She would speak softly, not looking up from what she was doing. I would pause grudgingly at the door, knowing what to expect but pausing anyway.

"Don't go too far in sin, Son. It's dangerous to keep on living the way you're living."

"Mom, can't you let me have just one day of peace and quiet without laying that religious junk on me!"

"Watch how you speak to me, Son, and remember that God's got His hand on you."

"Yeah, sure, Mom, you've only told me that a few hundred times before, Mom. Don't you think it might be a good idea to get off my back sometimes?"

"Just remember what I said. God's got His hand on your life. You remember that, Sammy."

And out the door I'd go in a puff of blue smoke, cussing her under every breath and half hoping she would hear it. As soon as I got to the car, I would turn up the radio so loud that it rattled the speakers and hurt my ears and kept me from thinking about what she had said.

Sometimes my rebellion got the best of her, and she lost that soft mother's kindness. Then the volume of our voices went up and our words became harsh and angry, and the distance between us grew.

But with everything else going so well, it was easy to dismiss this family disharmony as trifling and unimportant, and I plunged eagerly on into my new life in rock music.

CHAPTER 4

ONE NIGHT IN MARCH of 1966, when I least expected it, I got my chance to break into the big time.

The Mor-Loks were playing at a place called Tigers Den North, a teen discotheque in Miami. The occasion was a big dance sponsored by WQAM, Miami's top station for rock music. We were performing in a preliminary spot, warming up the crowd for the main attraction of the night, a Miami group called the Birdwatchers.

We were good that night. As usual, I did the vocal work, and I remember how responsive the kids were and how freely the music seemed to come. I stepped down off the side of the stage after we finished our set, and almost bumped into a handsome young man who stood waiting to talk to me.

"I'd like to talk with you for a few minutes," he shouted over the noise of his band tuning up onstage. "Can you wait around until we finish our first set?" Could I? You'd better believe I could, and did, and by the time he came back to talk with me a half hour later, I was hungrily anticipating what he wanted to see me about.

He came right to the point. "I like your voice, Sammy," he said, "and I think you have just the right sound to sing a new tune that we're recording. Would you like to give it a try?"

That was about like asking a monkey if he would like a banana. Of *course* I wanted to give it a try! He gave me the address of a Miami recording studio and said he would meet me there on Tuesday. The tune was a new one named "Girl, I've Got News for You." He had written it himself, and the group had recorded all but the vocal solo already.

The taping session was a great success and I never sang with the Mor-Loks again. The record was released the next week. It got lots of air-play by the Miami disc jockeys, and immediately took off on the local charts. The Bird-watchers, though one of Miami's best rock groups, had never had a hit record before, and the guys were delirious with the quick popularity of the release. They welcomed me into the group with open arms. I quit my job, resigned from the Mor-Loks, and just like that, I was the lead vocalist with Miami's top rock combo.

"Girl, I've Got News for You" continued to climb on the Top Forty charts. It began to get national interest, and *Billboard,* the top magazine of the recording industry, chose it as a national "pick hit." Within a few weeks it was the number one tune in Miami, and it stayed there for seven weeks.

Instant success. That's what the papers called it. I woke up one morning to find my picture in the Miami *Herald* and a story about the sudden change in my fortunes. Here's how the story began:

> Almost everything is coming in instant packages these days, including success. Take Fort Lauderdale's Sam Hall, for instance.
>
> Sam cut a record with the Birdwatchers before he had officially joined the group. After he had been singing with them for two weeks, the record, "Girl, I've Got News for You," was released and has been on the top ten record lists since then.
>
> That was six weeks ago and the record has since been released nationwide. To top it off, the Birdwatchers learned via telegram that the song was rated request #1 in Cincinnati. . . .

It was true. Success did come suddenly, maybe too suddenly for me to know how to handle it. I had been working as a carpenter's helper; three weeks later I was making four hundred dollars a week on stage. I had been a nobody, a loser; three weeks later I was in the papers, the recording magazines, a small celebrity. I had been a two-bit rock singer; three weeks later I was a recording artist with a national hit. I had been singing for high-school sock-hops; three weeks later I was playing the big-time nightclub circuit. Instant success? You'd better believe it, and nobody played the role to the hilt like I did.

The Birdwatchers were a thoroughly professional group. There were five of us. I was the vocalist; Bobby Piccitti, the organist and manager. Lead guitarist was Joey Murcia, a big guy, about 6'2", with dark hair and a quick temper. Jerry Schills played bass guitar; he was short and well-built with long, blonde hair. We had the best drummer in the business, Eddie Martinez, a likeable fellow of Cuban descent who played the drums better than anybody I've ever heard before or since.

The Birdwatchers were on the road about half the time, and when in Miami worked regularly at one of the nightspots. Our work was of two kinds: nightclub engagements, when we played to adult audiences all over the eastern United States, and rock concerts, when we played to crowds of teen-agers by the thousands, mostly in Florida.

When I joined the Birdwatchers, I was unexpectedly thrown into the world of the big time. On the road, we traveled constantly, hauling our equipment with us in a van if the distances were short, flying if they were long. Always on the go, always pushing to get to the next place on time.

At home we played six nights a week from 10:30 P.M. to 4:30 A.M., thirty minutes on and thirty minutes off. I'd get home about daylight, sleep until early afternoon, then just loaf, waste time, bar-hop, until time to go to the club again.

The rock concerts were what really turned me on, playing to the kids, seeing hundreds, sometimes thousands of them all hyped up, straining to be turned loose by the music. The people in the clubs came to drink and be entertained, but those kids came for the *music*. They came to be driven up the walls, to jump and scream and faint and writhe on a chaotic dance floor while we flogged them with our music. They were great crowds to work to.

We did some big gigs in '66 and '67. We appeared with the Beach Boys in the Miami Beach Convention Hall, with an audience of thirteen thousand screaming teen-agers going wild all night long. It was such a gas, singing that night, with those big amplifiers driving our sound out into the huge, pulsating crowd. I was so carried away with the whole scene, I could hardly stand still on the stage.

We played a gig in Atlanta with Brian Hyland and the Blues Magoos, in Daytona Beach with the Young Rascals, in Tampa with Roy Orbison, and always it was a repeat of the same thing. The big crowd, the big sound almost knocking me off the stage, the bright lights, the lines of teen-agers trying to get autographs. I loved every minute of it.

Rock music gets to be a pretty emotional thing, and sometimes we were almost torn to pieces by our fans. Girls would try to break down the dressing room door after a concert, or grab an arm or leg as we left the stage and refuse to let go.

We were playing in Orlando once to a crowd of six thousand. We had a number one record at the time, and the kids were really charged up. I was wearing leather moccasins that laced up to my knees. The girls who mobbed around the stage were reaching for me, trying to grab my laces. I was teasing them as I sang, standing just beyond their reach, and I made a fatal miscalculation: I turned my head to look back at the organist. One girl dived onto the stage, grabbed my foot and with a heave jerked me off my feet. Another grabbed another leg and in a flash I was down in the crowd, lying on my back across their shoulders, still clutching my microphone.

The crowd went wild, and around the stage near pandemonium broke loose. I was slapped, scratched, kissed, squeezed, and had my vest ripped off my back before the police arrived to tear me loose from the crowd and put me back on the stage. And those were my fans!

We worked hard to keep our reputation going. When we were on the road and not working every night, we would often find a place to set up our instruments and practice, sometimes jamming late into the night, working on new tunes, pushing each other to get better and better.

The work paid off. We were invited to appear on the Dick Clark TV show called "Where the Action Is," a nationwide ABC show that dominated the rock music field in the middle sixties. We taped our shows at the Eden Roc, one of the most sophisticated Miami Beach clubs, and got rave reviews on our performances.

We became one of the hottest properties in our area. We were scheduled to play a set as a preliminary to a big concert by the Dave Clark Five, at that time the rage of the English and American rock world. They failed to come up with a sufficient guarantee, so we didn't show. A few days later one of the Miami papers reported:

The Birdwatchers musical group would seem
to be the group to keep an eye on if you like to
play the game of predicting winners of the near
future. The Birdwatchers not only cut a big
figure with their work with "Where the Action
Is" during last week's taping at the Eden Roc—
their absence from the Dave Clark concert in
Fort Lauderdale earlier in the week made a lot
of fans unhappy.

The Birdwatchers were advertised as a supple-
mentary act on the Clark show but actually
never had the engagement confirmed with a required escrow deposit.

We read that story and howled with delight. When the
Birdwatchers could dim the lustre of the Dave Clark Five
by not appearing with them, then things were looking
great for us. We got more mileage out of not going than
we would have gotten by being there.

All the breaks seemed to go our way. When a Hollywood movie producer came to shoot a film on location in
Miami, he asked for the top rock group in the area. That
was us, hands down. Two days and a few thousand dollars
later we were signed up to play in a movie called *Wild
Rebels*, a low-budget flick about a car racer turned motor-
cycle bum turned rock singer. We got to play and sing in
the movie, and when it hit the theatres a couple of months
later with our name on the marquee, the requests for our
bookings went sky-high.

It was a lousy movie, by the way, though it was fairly

popular at the drive-ins and reportedly made lots of money. I still see it advertised occasionally in small towns or as part of double features, and I wouldn't walk across the street to watch it again. We all went to see it when it first came out. The acting was so bad and the production so poor that we left the theatre not knowing whether to blush or laugh. We laughed, as they say, all the way to the bank.

Our recording efforts began to pay off in spades. After that first smash success, we had two more big hits which climbed high on the charts, and almost everything we recorded was a money-maker.

The club work became more and more lucrative. We were playing dates in Chicago, Detroit, New York, Washington, Atlanta, all of Florida's big cities. Again we found ourselves in the papers, this time in the "Show Biz" column of the *Herald*:

> Latest Miami group—maybe the only Miami group—to join the New York discotheque Establishment is five rockers called the Birdwatchers. In some pop art get-ups designed by Coconut Grove's Pierre Perez, the Birdwatchers open July 1 at Sybil Burton's little place in Manhattan, the fabled Arthur.

Everything was going great, but the pace was killing me. We were in great demand and we were pushing to take advantage of every opportunity. I hadn't been with the Birdwatchers long when a customer came up to me one night and handed me some pills in an envelope. "You look tired," he said. "Take these. They'll make you feel better." Then he was gone, and I never saw him again, or knew who he was.

The next day we were up early, having played until 4:30 that morning, driving to Orlando in central Florida for a concert that night. I took the pills out of my pocket. They were amphetamines, known more commonly as bennies or uppers, stimulants which give the user a feeling of great energy, give him an up, a mild high. I hesitated for a moment, and popped them into my mouth. *What difference does it make?* I thought. *Anyway, I need them to keep going.*

Almost immediately, I felt better. When we arrived to set up for the concert, I felt like I could work all night. I was amazed at how good those little pills could make me feel. The next morning was a different story. When the up wore off, the down was worse than any alcoholic hangover I'd ever had. My eyelids felt like they weighed a thousand pounds each, and I was absolutely drained.

A couple of bennies is a little thing, I told myself, but deep inside I knew that it would not end there. I had a sense of sadness, of foreboding, that told me this was not the end of my drug usage. It was, in fact, barely the beginning. Once again I had crossed one of those invisible barriers, and there was no turning back now.

After that I popped pills regularly, taking uppers (amphetamines) to get things rolling when I was low or tired, and downers (barbiturates) to settle me down when I was strung so tight I couldn't relax. The pills go by many names: dexies, goof balls, red devils, yellow jackets, rainbows. They all spell trouble in the same way—producing dramatic changes in the user's energy, awareness, and activity level. The person who uses pills regularly gets on an emotional roller coaster that he cannot control, and life becomes a jagged series of wild highs and gloomy lows. Mixed with alcohol, the pills become even more unpredictable and dangerous.

Getting the stuff was no problem. Miami is a major distribution point for illegal drug traffic, and the nightclub where we worked had a reputation for being a hotbed for the market. On the road, I learned who pushed pills at each stop. Very often it was a bartender in the clubs where we worked; sometimes it was a customer; but always there was someone willing to sell.

From there I got into marijuana, usually depending on the same contacts as with the pills. Turning on was an accepted part of the culture that I was in now, and I smoked my first joint between sets one night without giving it a second thought. Weed, grass, pot, call it by any name, it was as common and easy to come by as a Miami parking ticket. I smoked it the first time simply because I was offered a hit, and after that because I liked it.

Pot began as kind of a social thing with me, smoking to be convivial and accepted, smoking at parties when everyone else was turning on. That approach didn't last long. I quit waiting for excuses to smoke, and got high just for the great feeling it gave me. I turned on between sets at the club, on the road between engagements, at my friends' apartments during the afternoons.

I remember a friend who had been burning pot for years said to me one night, "Sammy, when you start turning on by yourself, man, that's when you're getting hooked. That's when you're getting to be a lousy pothead!"

And so I was. Marijuana affects different people in different ways. Me, it made fuzzy-headed—couldn't think straight, couldn't remember anything. I was lucid one minute and spaced-out the next. All I could think about was that great, great feeling. I found that I could usually perform while I was high on pot; and, if anything, I thought it made me sing better. At least that's the way it seemed at the time.

That became the ultimate trip, turning on in the dressing room, hitting that stage still high as a kite, and letting it all hang out. The psychedelic lights, the music, the crowd, my head still light and flaky—while it was going on, I wanted it to last forever.

Once I decided to turn on during a recording session, so the other guys laid down the instrumental tracks and cleared out to let me work. They darkened the studio except for one small cone of light at my microphone, and I stood in the dark, eyes closed, strung out halfway between somewhere and nowhere, and moaned the lyrics into the mike. The tape turned out to be a pretty good one, and the record sold well. I never tried it again, though, because the pot dried out my throat, and when I listened to the record later, I didn't like the way it made me sound.

Sex was as big a part of my new world as the drugs and

the music. Among the teen-agers who follow the rock scene, there are always girls who are so slavishly devoted to the rock culture that they will give literally anything to be close to the stars. Anything includes their bodies.

Groupies they are called, these girls who hang around the hotel rooms, scheme and connive to get backstage, shout their propositions through the dressing-room doors. All to be a part of what's happening, to be close to the rock musicians and get a little piece of the action.

Sexual activity had not been one of my things before I got into rock music professionally, and at first I couldn't believe that so many young girls, really attractive girls, were available at every stop on the road. *Why not?* I thought. *You're doing everything else, so why not this too?* And so I did. Two nights here, a night there, and then out of town and I'd never see them again. There was never a long, serious affair, just lots of quick, cheap sex.

It wasn't only the teeny-boppers, either. The clubs we worked had their share of women on the prowl, always older than at the rock concerts, often married or divorced. But it was the same story: they thought of performers as being somebody special, and for us that made easy one-night pickups even easier. I got to where I spent half my time on stage checking out the audience for prospects.

One night I got more than I bargained for. I noticed a girl in the audience who was so beautiful, so classy, that she stood out from the crowd. *This chick I've got to meet,* I thought. I sent a waiter to her table with a note, asking if I could join her between sets.

I did, and she was even lovelier close-up. Her name was Jackie Merletti; she was an airline stewardess, and a former Miss Hialeah from that Miami suburb. She was in the nightclub that night on a fake identification card, since she was still underage by Florida law. I danced with her, asked her for a date, and she said yes.

Much later, under much different circumstances, she would figure prominently in my life. But a lot was to happen before then, and all I knew that first night at the club, as I belted out my lines from the stage and watched her across the room, was that she was different from any other girl I had ever known. She had class and style and I was determined to get to know her better.

My life as a rock musician rolled along at a furious pace, and I was telling myself how happy I was, how contented I was, how much I was enjoying myself. The sermons I had heard at the little Church of God as a child, the prayers and warnings of my mother, the tragic end of Freddy Turner, all those things seemed far away in a distant, fuzzy past.

We did a song in our show that was called "I Have No Worried Mind." It was a real crowd-pleaser at the teen concerts, and the lyrics stand out sharply in my mind:

> Long hair, tight pants,
> Love to dance, make romance,
> Baby, that's the only life for me!
> I'm flying high; I paint the town;
> I love this life; I get around,
> And I have no worried mind.

> This is me, and I won't change,
> And the things I do make me happy.
> I have no problems, I have no cares,
> And I have no worried mind.

I screamed those words into the microphone night after night, and for a while they were true. For a while I was able to bury myself in the music, the booze, the sex, the drugs, and shut out all my worries.

But not for long. I couldn't continue in the strain I was in, at the pace I was going, before things would start to unravel. And then those reckless, carefree words would become a painful lie, and would come back to haunt me.

CHAPTER 5

SOME PEOPLE THINK that all nightclubs are gleaming, glamorous places like the exotic spots you hear about in Las Vegas or Miami Beach.

Nothing could be further from the truth. We played all kinds, from the posh, sophisticated resort hotels to some of the grubbiest holes you've ever laid eyes on. And we met all kinds of people, and saw all kinds of things. It wasn't exactly your everyday, all-American job for a guy barely old enough to take a legal drink.

Our hair was long by the standards of that day, and we were constantly being hassled about it by some half-drunk customer. "Hey, sweetie," "Good evening, madam," "Get a haircut, you creepy fag"—those were the kinds of comments from inebriated patrons that we learned to ignore. Nobody is more belligerent than a jealous drunk, and we had to contend with our share of them. The guys without dates always seemed to resent the fact that women were attracted to us as performers, and that meant trouble for us.

We were doing an engagement at Key West during a time when a record of ours was really big. The audience was too large for the place to handle comfortably, so the dance floor was crowded, and there was lots of excitement and tension in the air. A young homosexual, obviously and shamelessly gay, started dancing with another guy, and made a real drunken spectacle of himself. We watched him from the stage, thought it was funny, and made a few remarks about it. One of his friends saw us making fun of him and didn't like it. I left the stage between sets, pushed through the crowd to the bathroom to comb my hair, and he followed me.

He never said a word. When I turned around from the mirror, all I saw was a big, hairy fist coming in fast. It was a single blow, but it was well-delivered, and it knocked me cold. When I came to my senses on the bathroom floor, the man was gone and blood was dripping off the end of my nose from a gash between my eyes that was an inch long and went clear to the bone. Needless to say, I didn't work for a couple of nights after that.

One night at a Miami club we were in the middle of a song when a man bolted suddenly across the dance floor with a pistol in his hand, firing wildly into the air, yelling incoherently about some punk and his wife.

I dropped the mike right on the stage and dived behind a big speaker. Eddie and Bobby jumped down behind the drums, Jerry behind the bass amplifier, and Joey made a mad dash for the dressing room door. False alarm. It turned out the guy was drunk and looking for another customer who wasn't in the house at the time. They got him calmed down, talked us back onto the stage, and it was business as usual.

We learned that when things got tense, the bouncer was our best friend. He was getting paid by the house to keep order, and that included taking care of the musicians. Many a bouncer had to bail me out of bad trouble, because I was never a match for most of the guys whose anger I provoked. I was still that skinny little kid that sang from the altar bench, remember? And my body, while it had grown some, was never anything to brag about. If it hadn't been for a few strategically placed bouncers here and there, I would have been killed a dozen times over.

Not that I went around looking for trouble. Sometimes it just dropped in my lap. One night things were going a bit-slow when a woman jumped out of her seat, walked onto the empty dance floor, and began taking her clothes off. The manager gave us a wink, so we kept playing, changing the rhythm to match her movements. It was an impromptu, amateur striptease.

When she got down to the last item of her underwear, one chivalrous gentleman in the audience could stand it no more. He had been drinking too much, and he charged across the floor to her as the Great Protector, dragging her back to her table to keep her from making a complete fool of herself. In the meantime she had dropped a twenty-dollar bill out of her clothes, and I left the stage to pick it up and take it to her.

The Great Protector looked up just in time to see me advancing to her table proffering the twenty-dollar bill. He thought I was insulting her, impugning her virtue, and he exploded on me in a rage. The bouncer got there before he could work me over very badly, or I would have been beaten to a pulp right then and there.

One bouncer was a particularly memorable one. He was a gigantic man, over three hundred pounds, a former professional wrestler, and he had a hair-trigger temper. He was like a keg of dynamite with a short fuse. Once I saw him walk up to a drunk who was harassing another customer, spin him around without warning and hit him four straight times in quick succession. The guy's face just exploded, and they carried him out, streaming blood.

Another bouncer carried a pistol and shot an eighteen-year-old boy in the club parking lot one night. The kid started a fight, the bouncer said, and the shot was fired during the scrap. The same guy once fired a shot inside the club while we were singing and blew a hole the size of a man's fist in the wall over the bar. Like I said, I'm glad the bouncers were on our side.

The worst place we ever worked was a club in Chicago which turned out to be a real dive. The manager disliked us from the first night, complained about our instruments being too loud, hassled us about the raucous stuff we played. We figured if he didn't like rock music, he shouldn't have signed up a rock group, so we ignored his protests and blasted away. When time came to leave, he flatly refused to pay us. One of the guys in the group had a brother on the Chicago police force. We gave him a call; he came over; and, standing on the sidewalk in front of the joint, he got our money for us, literally at the point of a gun. Doesn't sound too glamorous, does it?

The teen concerts I liked better. They seemed some-how more innocent, more like fantasy-world, with all those adoring fans who thought we could do no wrong. It is unbelievable the ways the kids get attached to a group. We got a steady stream of letters and gifts from female fans. One young teen-age girl almost worshiped us. She refused to eat anything or get out of bed until one of us came to see her. Her older sister finally came to us in desperation and told us the story. We went to the girl's house, visited a few minutes, and she seemed satisfied, resuming then her normal life. Weird? Yes, but similar things happen constantly in the rock cult.

At first I was too carried away with the excitement of it all to think seriously about what I was doing. Sometimes the kids would get so excited and the music and emotion so intense that fights would break out spontaneously in the audience, especially if the kids were standing or danc-ing rather than sitting. Fights were common at big rock shows, and knifings were not at all rare.

At first I thought the whole scene was great. *Watch us turn these kids on*, I said to myself. *We are really driving these kids wild!* But as time went on, my delight with the power of our music gave way to troublesome, nagging worries about the rightness of it all, about what we were really doing to those kids to make them fight, make them so ready to have sex with us, to want to leave town and run away from home with us. When I was singing I could forget all that, but when I lay awake at night I couldn't dismiss those thoughts so easily, and they began to whis-per in my mind more and more loudly.

Since I had joined the Birdwatchers, several things had happened to remind me that I had not escaped the scrutiny of God's eye. Somehow I just couldn't shake God loose, no matter how I tried. The first of these occasions came on a Christmas Day, when all the family had gathered at home for the holidays.

It was midafternoon. The house was crowded and noisy, with all the family there, when Dad told me rather abruptly that he wanted to talk with me—privately. I could tell from his tone that he meant business, so we went outside and sat in the car to talk.

"Sammy," he began, "God has spoken to me about you, and I want you to hear me out."

I couldn't believe what I was hearing. Was that my dad talking? My old fishing buddy, my easygoing dad, who had never nagged me about religion in my life, even when he knew I was living a rotten and sinful life? Was that my dad talking, my dad who had never forced God on me, who acted sometimes as if he liked church as little as I did?

"I didn't want to tell you this, Son, but I haven't been able to sleep for a week. I've been all torn up, and I've got to tell you." He blinked hard and his eyes began to water, and with a big effort he continued: "God spoke to me in a vision a few nights ago. I know it sounds funny coming from me, but I'm just telling you what happened as sure as we're sitting here.

"I was in a big hurricane wind, and all of a sudden the wind stopped and it was dead quiet. Then a voice spoke and I knew it was God. The voice said, 'Your grandson will never grow up. Your son will go young.' And then I woke up. I don't know much about what you're doing, Son, but I know you're not living for God. I'm begging you, Sammy, please give up the way you're living and make your peace with God before it's too late."

His voice was choked with emotion, and when he stopped there was not a sound in the car but the beating of our two hearts. I was numb. Stunned. Didn't know what to say, how to respond, so I just sat and looked dumbly at the dashboard, not seeing it, not seeing anything, until he left the car and went back into the house.

If that message had come from anyone else, I would have shrugged it off, but it didn't, and I couldn't. It came from my dad, and it hit me like a Mack truck. It scared me right down to my innards, and it stuck down there somewhere, and I never did get it out.

That incident was still fresh in my mind months later when I got a phone call that penetrated my super-cool front and broke me up like a stale cookie. I was in Daytona Beach, playing a big concert there. We were just about to go onstage when the call came, long distance from my brother-in-law in Ocala, a town in the central part of the state. I was all juiced up, ready to perform, and almost didn't take the call.

I answered the phone with that all-right-I'm-in-a-hurry-what-do-you-want voice that you use when you want the guy on the other end of the line to make it short and to the point.

"Sammy, I'm calling from the hospital here in Ocala. We brought Jeff in for tests a day or two ago because

he's not been well lately. We just got the results back
. . . he's got acute leukemia."

He paused for a moment. It was my nephew he was
talking about, my four-year-old nephew, Jeff Decker.
"The doctors say it's terminal, Sammy, and they don't
think there's much they can do. All the family is here, and
we want to know if you can come to see Jeff?"

I hung up. Maybe I said something, maybe I didn't, I
don't know. I just don't know. I sagged against the wall,
then walked woodenly, blindly, out onto a patio which
was built off the backstage area of the auditorium. *Jeff is
going to die,* I thought. I slumped into a chair and tried
to light a cigarette. *Jeff is going to die,* the thought
echoed, and not all the clamorous, deafening noise from
the concert inside could drown it out.

I played that night at Daytona Beach, hardly knowing
what I was doing. We were scheduled to do a concert at
the University of Florida in Gainesville the next night,
and Ocala was not a very long drive from there, so the
next afternoon found me pulling my car into the hospital
parking lot, and heading for the children's wing on the
fourth floor.

My nephews had always been very close to me, especially Jeff. He was the son of Vonceil, my next oldest sister.
I thought of how I loved him and was proud of him, how
he used to beg me for ice cream whenever he visited my
house, how he liked to go with me to play putt-putt golf,
and how thrilled he was when I let him hit the ball. I
remembered the times I had to spank him when he stayed
with me, and how I hated to do it, and how mean I felt
afterward.

And now he was going to die, and however much I dodged the idea, I kept coming back to it: *it's your fault, Sammy. God is doing this to tell you something.* That doesn't make sense, I told myself. God wouldn't do that. But I remembered my rebellion and my stubbornness and how flagrantly I was sinning against God every day, and I couldn't shake the nagging, tormenting guilt out of my mind.

When I arrived, all the family was there, standing and sitting around the bed where Jeff sat, surrounded by toys of every imaginable description. He alone was cheerful and happy that afternoon. For the rest of us, it was a bleak, dingy day. I had brought my guitar to sing for Jeff, who was always one of my best fans. I played and sang and tried to be as bright as possible. I thought, *everyone else here is praying for Jeff—all I can do is sing him a few stupid songs.*

I stayed as late as I could stay and still make it to Gainesville for the concert that night. Finally I had to leave, to tell him goodbye, to walk down those stinking-sterile hospital halls, my eyes full of tears, blindly hating whatever put my nephew on his back in that awful formaldehyde-smelling place.

That night I sang to the huge university crowd and while I worked I made promises to God by the bushelful. I was singing and praying all at once and the songs' insane lyrics and my mind's desperate thoughts made a bizarre weave that night. *Please, God, heal Jeff!* . . . "Baby, won't you come on and love me" . . . *I'll do anything, God, if you'll heal Jeff* . . . "The whole world's groovin' outasight tonight" . . . *No more liquor, God, I swear, no more liquor*

... "I'm the life of the party, can't you see" ... *No more drugs, no more sex, God, I'm through, God* ... "And I have no problems, I have no cares, I have no worried mind."

We drove back to southern Florida the next day, and those promises didn't last through the day. In the weeks that followed, I plunged in deeper and deeper, and in my rebellion against God, I hurled in His face those promises made on the Gainesville stage. When I thought of Jeff, and the aching came back, I soaked it in the sounds of my music until I felt it no more.

Jeff lived for quite a while longer, his condition growing steadily worse. One morning he woke up completely blind, and two months later he died.

I had passed the point of no return. My pill-popping increased, and I stayed on grass so much that I was becoming a chronic pothead. Drugs I had never tried before, I tried now. I started to mix things with marijuana to give it a little extra kick. First came DMT, a hallucinogenic drug, then cocaine and morphine.

Methedrine is one of the most potent stimulant drugs available. Speed is what they call it, for the rushing sensation it gives. Speed-freaks are some of the most messed-up people in the whole drug scene, but I ignored that and soon found that I could trip on speed with a bigger kick than with anything I had used before. I tried to get high on glue, without much luck, so I sniffed other things, paint thinner, gasoline, certain nasal decongestants, anything that I thought would get me high.

My good experiences with DMT led me to experiment with other hallucinatory drugs, something I had told myself earlier I'd never do. I tripped out so much that every minute I wasn't high on something I was in a blue funk, depressed, despondent, suicidal.

My plunge into serious drug abuse led me to excesses in other areas as well. We were playing a club in Chicago, a nice place right off Lakeshore Drive, when we met a fellow whom we knew to be a pusher in Miami. He invited me to a party at his apartment, only a few blocks away. I went, and by the middle of the morning everyone there was stoned out of his mind.

It developed into a full-blown orgy, with perverts, homosexuals, everybody there doing his own thing. People were dancing in the nude. I was high as a kite, and at the time it seemed like great fun. I woke up about sunrise, saw everybody passed out all over the apartment, draped over couches and chairs, and I was so disgusted with myself and the whole sordid mess that I could hardly stand it. I felt like crying; I felt like screaming; I felt like dying. I was sick of myself and what I had become. I left the place as soon as I could get myself together, and spent the morning walking through the Chicago streets in a cold, spitting snow.

Professionally, the Birdwatchers were doing better than ever. We put out another hit record, a tune called "Mary, Mary." It was a love song to marijuana, and not surprisingly, the kids ate it up:

Mary comes along in the darkness of the night,
Sneaks up on me and she makes things alright.
Mary makes me feel like I'm comin' on strong,
Mary makes me happy when the cards are fallin' wrong.
Whatever you may say, Mary's here to stay!

The irony of the song was not lost on me—my life was on the skids that drugs put under my feet, and here I was singing the praises of marijuana.

The big money was coming in, up to $800 a week on the good weeks, and the sky seemed to be the limit. I paid for a brand-new Pontiac without batting an eye. We got top billing in almost every rock concert we worked, and disc jockeys all over the state were giving each new record we put out lots of air-play. We all had dreams of what it would be like to become a national smash-hit group.

But through it all, I was miserable and unhappy. I got to where I had a pervasive feeling of loneliness; even when I was with four of five people, I felt alone. I was never happy except for the few hours each night that we were playing and the music was really cooking. Once the editor of a high-school newspaper interviewed me and asked if I were truly happy. I remember his surprise when I told him no. I didn't make any explanation; I just looked right at him and said "No," just like that.

I told myself that my unhappiness came from craving more of what I had a taste of—more of "the good life," more drugs, more sex, more popularity. I tried to talk myself into being an atheist, and denied vehemently that religion had anything to do with my lack of contentment.

Just give me more of what I've got, I said, and I'll be happy.

It was clear what was happening. The more I got of the things I was chasing, the unhappier I became. I had taken my life into my own hands, wrenched myself away from God, and was charging headlong down a dead-end street. And now it was time for God to bring me back.

Sammy with little friend at age 2

Sammy at age 3

Blueberry Fields Forever
Sammy and sister Judy singing at age 8

Sammy Hall Singer —
with sisters Voncile & Bernice

The Sammy Hall Group —
(L-R top) Jeff, Roeina, Sue
(L-R front row) Sammy, Mike, Lenny Sattler

The Mor-Loks—#1 group in Florida 1963-1965

Our first bus — WOW!

Monte's on his way.

The Birdwatchers — 1966-1969

The Birdwatchers 1967
Sammy Jerry, & Bobby

The Birdwatchers — 1968
Bobby, Sammy, Joey, Jerry, Eddie

The Birdwatchers — 1968
Bobby, Samm6y, Joey, Eddie, Jerry

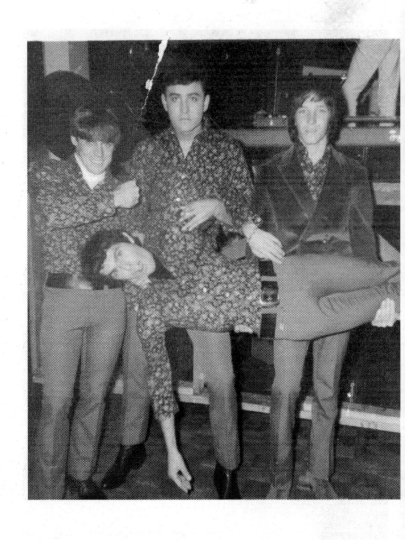

The Birdwatchers — backstage

Jackie, National Airline 1968

CHAPTER 6

IT WAS FEBRUARY 17, 1968, and it was a typical Saturday night at the club.

To be the most important day of my life, it certainly had an ordinary beginning. I had slept until two in the afternoon, fixed myself breakfast, and before I could get out of the house I had gotten into an argument with my mother. (I had kept an apartment for awhile, but was out of town so much with the Birdwatchers that I decided to move back in with my parents, even if it meant putting up with an occasional sermon from Mom.)

Believe me, the sermons had never stopped. I might be a big deal to some people, but to her I was still just a wayward boy, and she persisted in bending my ear whenever she could. As I became well-known around Miami, the phone calls from female fans became more frequent, and sometimes the come-on was too explicit for even my mother to misunderstand.

Teen-age girls came by the house to holler from the road or knock at my window occasionally, and this infuriated her. Late one night a girl tried to crawl through my bedroom window, mistakenly chose my parents' window instead, and awakened what surely must have been the most irate, most indignant mother in Broward County. At any rate, the situation at home was lousy, as usual, and this particular morning, having little patience with my mother's concern, I had left the house in a huff.

We started playing at 10:30 P.M. for the crowd that was in the club that night, and I remember that our performance was a very good one. It was the standard Birdwatchers scene: Bobby in the back, firmly massaging the organ, Eddie slavering over his drums, his hands never still, Joey fondling the long-necked guitar slung low across his body, Jerry hunched over the bass, hungrily rooting out the notes, and me out on the edge of the stage, soaking up that sweet spotlight, microphone held against my mouth, slipping the words out to the people one at a time.

It is important to remember just what condition I was in at the time. Professionally, things could not have been better; but physically and emotionally, I was at the end of my rope. My mind was stretched and blown; instead of developing a tolerance for the drugs I was using, I was going crazy, getting higher every time I turned on. I was having some unbelievable hallucinations, and my nerves were unraveling fast.

Doing more and enjoying it less—that about describes my situation. Nothing seemed to stop the hunger inside me for whatever it was that I didn't have. I was engaged to Jackie Merletti at the time, but was always restless, always running around, always looking for more action.

Between sets that night I spent some time with an attractive girl who had been hanging around the club for the past few weeks. She was an airline stewardess, and I had several drinks with her between midnight and closing time. She had the reputation of being a speed-freak, and easy to go to bed with, so when she asked me to give her a drive home after we finished our last set, I was only too eager to offer my services. We left the club at about 4:45 A.M.

As we pulled up outside the apartment complex where the girl lived, she suggested that we turn on. Sure. Why not? Her roommate was asleep inside, so we sat there in the parked car as she pulled several joints out of her purse. They looked like ordinary marijuana joints, but she assured me that it wasn't grass alone, but a special mixture. "A little bit of everything" was the way she put it.

We sat there smoking for a long time, and the drug began to affect me in a strange, scary way that I had never experienced before. I decided I'd better get on the road before I got too zonked to drive, so she told me goodnight and went inside, and I headed for home.

As I drove through Miami, headed toward Fort Lauderdale, I suddenly lost all knowledge of where I was; my mind began to go blank, and I couldn't remember anything. It was spooky. Street names that I should have known looked strange and unfamiliar. I was lost in a city that I knew like the back of my hand, just wandering through the streets like a child in a strange place. I couldn't remember where I had been, or where I was going.

Suddenly, after what seemed an eternity, I snapped out of it, and found myself barreling along the highway toward Homestead Air Force Base, headed south, on the opposite side of the city from where I wanted to go. I got the shakes when I realized how long I had apparently been out of control behind the wheel. Turning the car around, I headed north again and soon was out of downtown Miami on my way toward home.

My mind started to rush now, and I began to have the sensation of time and space streaming over me in wave after wave of some eerie supernatural current. I had the feeling of tremendous velocity, like the car was hurtling along the road at breakneck speed. I clutched the steering wheel grimly, badly frightened by the motion of the car which I couldn't control, but when I looked down at the speedometer, it said twenty miles per hour. Then things outside would float by for awhile in slow motion, like the car was barely moving, and I would see the speedometer saying eighty. My mind was going haywire, and I didn't know what was real and what was illusion.

As I drove along, I realized that I was separating into two beings, each strangely apart from the other, one sitting on top of the car looking down at the other one inside, and I was both of them. It was bizarre and agonizing, and I wondered where I could go for help. *Nowhere,* I told myself, *just keep driving, just get home and you'll be all right.*

I had been spaced out pretty badly before, but somehow, fuzzily, I realized that this was different, this was going to be worse, and I was going to be in real trouble.

I felt fragmented, like I was breaking apart into thousands of pieces, and I would never be able to get them together again.

I had to talk to somebody, anybody, even a stranger, just to get in touch with some kind of reality. There was a gas station just up the road, and I pulled off to the right and into the driveway. I got out, fumbled in my pockets for a dime, pushed it into the slot, and got a soda. I hoped that the sensation of the cool liquid would help me down somehow, at least enough to get me home. I stood there and looked into my car, standing with the door open, afraid like a little baby to get back into it and drive down the road into the dark and the unknown. I started talking to the attendant. It felt good just to be talking to someone; it was reassuring not to be alone. I thought I was making sense, but I must have been so flipped out that it scared him, because he just looked at me, backed nervously away, and shouted for me to leave.

I got back into the Pontiac and took off. I was a short distance down the road when I started hearing the wind howl around me, a strong, whining wind right there inside the car. I could feel demons in my car, could almost see them, swarming all over me. I looked over to the passenger's seat and could see Satan materializing there, in and out of focus, blurred and distorted. I screamed, "Help me, please, somebody help me!" yelling at the top of my voice, over and over.

The next thing I knew, the car was pulled off the road, motor still on, and I was out of the car, running, stumbling, scrambling down the shoulder of the highway. I didn't know, didn't care where I was going; I just wanted to get away from my car, away from the heart-stopping fear that was there. I fell, got up, fell, got up again, and finally stood, gasping for breath, looking back at the automobile. I was confused, my mind flying past at a thousand miles an hour, and I couldn't get it to stop.

Then the voice came. Loud, demanding, overpowering. "Sammy, take your life." I looked all around me, turning in a bewildered circle, dazed and shaken. Again it came, commanding me, driving me, "Sammy, take your life." I remembered my dad's warning, and I had a feeling of destiny working itself out, slowly, fatally, giving no quarter, demanding that it was my time to die.

The voice came again, and I was obsessed with the need to obey. I ran back to the car and began to search for a pen, pencil, screwdriver, anything sharp to stab myself with. I had to die; it had to happen; I wanted to hurry it up, to do it, to get it over with. I looked everywhere, tore the console open in the front, jerked the back seat off its mountings. I knelt on the road, frantic, clawing through the junk on the back floor, looking for something with which to obey the voice.

Unable to find any sharp object in the car, I got to my feet and started across the road. I had just passed a hamburger joint, maybe a quarter of a mile back, and vaguely remembered that it was open all night. I thought I could go back to it and find something to do the job with. As I crossed the road, I saw a police car

pull out of the darkness onto the highway and head toward me, so I ran back to my car, got inside, and as the
patrol car passed by, I pulled slowly onto the road behind
it.

In a flash, the police car vanished into thin air. It had
been a hallucination all along, suddenly it was gone, and
with a jolt my mind came back. I started coming down,
shaking so badly that I had my knees and elbows on the
steering wheel to help guide the barely moving Pontiac.

For the first time in my life, I prayed a serious prayer,
a prayer with no conditions, a prayer that came out of
desperate, aching need. I screamed out to God, confessing
my sins, begging for forgiveness, asking God to show me
if He was real and if He was hearing my prayer. *Please,
God, show me that you are there. I beg you, God, to let me
feel your presence. Show me you are real, God!* I felt
nothing but my racing heart, heard nothing but my own
voice rattling and echoing in the car.

I remember thinking that I was going crazy, that I was
actually going insane. I thought how cruel, how terrifying
to watch my mind disintegrate and be aware of what is
happening and be able to do nothing about it. *I'm going
crazy*, I thought, *but I'm going to kill myself first.*

My mind started to rush again, and the fear set in again,
and again I felt compelled to die. My foot jammed down
against the accelerator, and the car leaped ahead. I tried
to lift my foot off the pedal, but it wouldn't respond. I was
separating again, half of me grimly determined to die, half
praying fervently to live. I couldn't move, could only
watch, horror-stricken, as the auto gained speed and
headed for the side of the road.

Once more I tried to pray. *Please, God, help me!* I began to cry, loud, wracking sobs, tears running freely down my face. I remember saying, *Look, God, I'm humble, I'm crying, I mean business.*

And just as suddenly as it all had started, it was over. A warm glow began to flood over me as Jesus Christ came into my life and God's Holy Spirit possessed my body. In a fantastic surge that I've never found a way to describe, all the empty frustration of my life dissolved, and I knew that I was free from the misery that had bound me for years.

The presence of God in the car was so real that I never doubted what had happened to me. It was cool and damp outside, and I remember checking to see if the car heater was on, so strong was the sensation of warmth which accompanied His spirit. The daylight began to break as I drove home, the most beautiful, clean, sunrise I've ever seen; and I drove along crying, praying, thanking God every minute of the way.

What happened to me that night was incredible! Absolutely incredible! Even now when I tell it, it sounds like science fiction, or a bad dream, or a madman's tale. But it was real, every moment of it, just as I have described it. I was stubborn; I was headstrong; and I had to go to the thin edge of death before I would bow my will to God. But when I was willing to surrender to God my whole life, with nothing held back, no questions asked, He accepted me like a loving Father embracing a stricken son.

I pulled my car into the driveway at home as the sun came up, and walked into the house, exhausted. I don't know much about theology. I don't know much about psychology. But I was sure of one thing then, as I am sure of it now: the Sammy Hall who fell into bed that morning was not the Sammy Hall who had climbed out of it the day before. This Sammy Hall was a new, different man. He was a child of God, and he could never be the same again.

CHAPTER 7

I WOKE UP THREE HOURS LATER feeling clearheaded and rested.

I'm the kind of guy who usually wakes up one piece at a time; getting me fully awake is about a thirty-minute process. This time it was different. I opened my eyes and was wide awake immediately.

I lay in bed for a minute or two, revelling in the peace and serenity that I felt inside. It was such a new experience for me that I literally lay there and wallowed in that great, relaxed feeling of spiritual freedom to which I was so unaccustomed.

I listened to the sounds of dishes banging and feet shuffling in the kitchen as Mom and Dad got breakfast and prepared to leave for Sunday School. *I won't tell them right now,* I decided. I was eager for them to believe me when I told them that I had been born again, and I figured I had a few details to settle before I could let them know.

As soon as they left the house, I bounced out of bed and headed for the shower. For the first time in my life, I wanted to go to church; I looked forward to getting there. When I walked in the door just about the time service started, heads turned in my direction, and huge question marks shot across the faces of my mom and dad.

It was a curious occasion for me, that first worship service after I accepted Christ. It was the same little Pentecostal church that I had attended and hated so many times as a boy—same people, same style of worship, same everything. But this morning it all seemed different, like I was wired up differently, so that the vibes I got were good ones, and the singing, the preaching, the prayers, all of it seemed rich and good. The same setting that had provoked such hostility from me before provoked a sense of worship that morning.

There was a little old lady in the church who had been my self-appointed conscience for the last several years. Running into her was like meeting my mother-away-from-home. She would grab my hands and tell me that she was burdened for me, praying for me, "holding me up before the Lord," as she always put it. I detested that, and despised her for it. I remember seeing her in the service that morning and feeling a sense of gratitude and love, a sudden affection for her that was strong and moving.

I still had some big problems, and as I listened to the preacher preach, I wondered how they would be resolved. The first thing I had to do was get out of rock music, out of show business altogether. I had to resign from the Birdwatchers and kiss the whole entertainment bag goodbye. God didn't have to speak to me and tell me that. I just knew that accepting Christ meant giving up my job with the group.

Somehow it never even crossed my mind that there was any other choice. My career as a singer was so completely intertwined with sin, so shot through with liquor and sex, drugs and violence, that I knew I could not stay in that life and remain a Christian. In fact, it is feeling that way that kept me away from God so long. I longed for peace and fulfillment but I knew that I couldn't serve God and keep my career as a rock musician too, and I just didn't have the guts to give it up. When I finally said yes to Jesus in my car the night before, I knew that I was making the decision then and there to leave the Birdwatchers for good.

Now, as I sat soberly on the pew, I wondered if I could actually do it—if I would have what it took to make a clean break with the old life. As the preacher went on, I prayed quietly there in the pew. I prayed slowly, awkwardly, picking my words carefully because I didn't know quite how to pray. I asked God for guidance and strength, to help me resign from the group and make a complete about-face in my life.

When the service was over, I went home for lunch with my folks and we ate without much conversation. They made no comment about my going to church, and when I left the house in midafternoon, I still had made no attempt to answer their unspoken questions.

We had double engagements that night, with a teen concert scheduled for the early evening in South Miami, and our regular gig at the club later on. Maybe other people would have done it differently, but I played both those dates. I had mixed emotions about what to do, but figured I was doing the right thing. I didn't drink, smoke, or turn on, but I sang with the group as usual, and it was really a strange feeling. On the one hand, I felt miserable. The whole scene was suddenly stale and distasteful, and none of the old excitement was there. On the other hand, I felt great. I would sit around between sets thinking about what the Lord had done for me, and I was wonderfully, indescribably happy.

We had a tune that we had just recorded called "Weeping Analeah." It was a very popular song, and as I sang it to the kids at the concert that night, I was struck by the aptness of one of the verses:

> Well, yesterday's gone forever and ever
>   and never to be again
> Oh, you look for the sunshine
> That brought warmth to your mind

The lyrics go on and on nonsensically, but that little slice of music seemed to be talking to me, and I played it and replayed it in my mind.

Monday was our off night, so it was no problem. All day Tuesday I worried about what I should do that night. To sing or not to sing. I finally decided to sing, jumped into my car and got to the club in time for the first show. The same thing happened all over again Wednesday.

By Thursday I was getting uptight about the situation. Here it was four full days since my conversion experience, and still I had told no one about it, and was still singing to a houseful of drunks until four o'clock every morning. I told the Lord I thought it was time for me to make my move, and asked him a few hundred more times to help me. *Here goes, Lord,* I thought, *I sure hope you know what we're doing.*

That night at the club, the whole band got into a huge fuss. There had been some misunderstanding about expenses on the road, and the way some of the money had been handled. It was nickel and dime stuff, really, but somehow it got all blown out of proportion, and we ended up in a knockdown, drag-out squabble.

The whole scene was a first for us. We had practically lived together for two years, and had always gotten along great together. Our personalities had grooved like a charm. I mean, we hardly ever even argued, much less had a big fight over something as two-bit as this was.

It was the opportunity I had been waiting for—just the opening I needed to overcome my reluctance and make a break. So, right then and there, I told the guys I was pulling out.

Later in the night, I talked to Bobby between sets and told him I really was resigning, that I was serious about leaving the group. I told him that I was unhappy, that I had been unhappy for a long time. I said that I had decided to leave the business and try to get a new life started away from the drugs and night life.

He looked at me long and solemnly, and I think he understood. "Okay, Sammy," he said with a resigned sigh. "Okay, man. I think you're crazy, but okay." There was no argument, no appeal, no questions, and I really think he understood. "Just work out a two-weeks notice," he said, "and we'll try to find a new boy to take your place."

When that was done, the burden lifted for me, and I knew that I was going to make it.

The next day I got up and told Mom the double news: I have been born again, and I have resigned from the Birdwatchers. She cried and rejoiced and hugged me and, I suspect, got on the phone to her friends as soon as I was out the door. After telling her, I left the house and went straight to my dad's produce market. I found him there cleaning up behind the market, and told him the whole story.

I was eager for my brother and sisters to know what had happened to me. They had prayed for me for years, and I had always been the prodigal, the black sheep. Now I was eager for them to hear of my conversion. Mom took care of that by phone in short order. It had not been very long before that Vonceil, the mother of my nephew Jeff, had felt specially burdened to pray for me. I had flown from a nightclub engagement in Detroit into Orlando, where she and her husband were living, and she had met me to tell me of her urgent concern. Such things were annoying and bothersome at the time, but now that I had found God, they brought me even closer to my family.

But the biggest hurdle of all still remained. Jackie Merletti. What would Jackie say? She knew nothing about my church background, nothing about the new birth, had no idea of the spiritual struggle that had gone on inside me.

Jackie and I had dated often since that first night we met. We had learned to love each other, and agreed that we would be married as soon as I got off the nightclub circuit. I had always felt that I couldn't be faithful to a wife while I was working the clubs. She was still working as a stewardess, and I was on the road half the time, so we agreed not to get married until I was ready to settle down and stay at home more of the time.

I left my dad's market for Jackie's apartment, wondering all the way what kind of reaction to expect.

When I got there, I came right to the point. "I'm quitting the Birdwatchers," I said. "I've accepted Jesus Christ as my Saviour, and I'm giving up my job as a singer."

Jackie hit the ceiling! It was the craziest thing she'd ever heard of, she said. It was just like throwing my life away, she said. What would I do with myself? How could I ever make a living? How could I become so all-fired religious all of a sudden? Preposterous, outrageous, and totally out of the question, she said.

I let the outburst subside and tried again to explain what had happened. It took a long time, a lot of filling in, supplying background about my church and what we believed and what we practiced. Jackie had been a Methodist, but in name only, and frankly admitted knowing nothing about the new birth, and nothing at all about the daily exercise of Christian discipleship.

I couldn't answer all of her questions that day; certainly I couldn't counter all of her arguments. She believed that my decision was an impulsive reaction to a bad drug trip, and that I would be sorry later if I gave up my job. "Tell them you've changed your mind," she urged, and when I refused she called me a stubborn fool and threatened never to see me again. When I left her apartment to go to the club, she was still angry and crying.

That night was only the first night of my two-weeks notice with the Birdwatchers. The entire nightclub thing had become a real bummer to me since Saturday night. I seriously wondered if I could stand to sing there for two full weeks, the atmosphere had become so unsavory to me. I need not have worried. God took care of the problem by making me sick.

You ask, would God actually make a person sick? Well, I don't know about most of the time, but I am convinced that He did *that* time. After working only one night of the two weeks, I got sick, really, genuinely sick, too sick to work until the two weeks were over, and I was free of the Birdwatchers completely. They were good friends and they treated me right. But God had given me a new life, and it had no room in it for my old habits.

There was one remaining tie with my rock-music past that had not been severed: my recording contracts. The records I had cut with the Birdwatchers would continue to sell, of course, but I had nothing to do with that anymore. There was another recording contract that was more of a problem. In my last few months with the Birdwatchers, I had made a couple of records as a solo artist, released under my own name rather than with the group. The label I was working with was Parrott Records, the British company that was making international stars out of Tom Jones and Engelbert Humperdinck at about that time.

Parrott was enthusiastic about the marketing prospects of my stuff, and had called me in to cut a tape the week of my conversion. The record was getting lots of prerelease raves, including a selection by *Billboard* as a "can't miss" prospective hit. Just as I debated whether or not I was doing the right thing by allowing the tune to be released, Parrott asked me to come in to help them put together a big promotional campaign for it.

I didn't know what to do. No harm, I figured, in letting them release the record. But still I didn't feel right about it. I wanted to break every tie with rock music, and I was afraid that the recording contract might be the little thing that would lure me back in later on.

While I was sick in bed, the week after I gave Bobby Piccitti my resignation, I had lots of time to think and pray. I wanted to give God a chance to speak to me in a way that I could know His will. I decided to ask God to give me a Christian song, a song of testimony, and I would accept that as a message to drop the recording. If it's all right to go ahead with the record, just don't do anything, I would tell Him.

When I prayed, it was early afternoon, and I got more emphatic in my prayer than I had planned. When I got into the heart of my prayer, I tacked "today" onto the end of the deal. "If you don't give me a song *today*, Lord, I'll go ahead with the record release," I prayed. "Give me a song *today*, Lord."

And that is just what happened. I have written many religious songs since that one, but I've never had one given to me like that one was. "God Plus Nothing Equals Everything" was what I called it, and it virtually wrote itself as the Lord inspired me to copy it down. It was another direct answer to prayer, and it bolstered my faith greatly at a time of real need.

A few days later I walked into the recording office, asked for a release from my two-year contract, and got it. There was a clause that gave me the right to choose my own selections for recording, and when I told them that I wouldn't do anything but sacred music anymore, they were not at all reluctant to let me out of the contract.

I was really a displaced person those first few weeks after my conversion. I had been a night person, accustomed to sleeping until early afternoon and staying up almost until daylight. I had no job, was not in school, and worked with my dad at the produce market until I could find steady work.

I got my first chance to witness during that time. Wanting to be alone, I went down to the park in Fort Lauderdale, broke out my guitar, and began to play and sing softly to myself. There was a group of longhairs nearby, and they started to turn on, passing joints around the circle from one to the other. They asked me to join them, and I told them thanks, but it wasn't for me anymore. Why not, they wanted to know. And I told them the whole thing about how Christ had changed my life, and how I didn't need that stuff anymore. It was my first time to witness, and it fell right into my lap.

Meanwhile, Jackie was coming slowly to accept my decision. She still didn't understand what had happened, but she understood that I loved her very much, and that I was doing what I felt I had to do. She also understood that I needed her support if I was going to make it. She didn't like it, and she certainly was not ready to swallow the religious bit yet, but she decided she cared for me enough to stick it out.

I said I wanted to marry her, and she said okay. I said soon, and she said okay. I said like next week, and she *still* said okay. And so we were to be married, a scant four weeks after my conversion.

On the night before the wedding, I came very close to blowing the whole thing. Some of my old friends had heard about the wedding, and threw a party in my honor. Things just started to get into gear when somebody hauled out the grass and DMT, and everybody started to turn on.

A friend handed me a joint. *Well, just tonight,* I thought, *just once more for old times' sake.* The party was being given for me, after all; the whole thing was in my honor. I took three or four hits on that joint and it about blew the top right off my head.

What was wrong with me? I was getting zonked on a few puffs of pot! The room started to spin lazily around, I couldn't focus my eyes on anything. I held my head between my hands and felt like screaming. For one terrifying second I thought that I had sinned and God had left me for the last time. The thought shot panic through my heart.

I jumped up, said goodbye to no one, dashed out the door, down the stairs, into my car, and headed home. As I drove I asked God to forgive me for my carelessness, for my foolish lapse. The next day Jackie and I were married, and I've never come that close to going back on drugs since.

So there I was, a newly married man without a house, a high-school diploma, or a steady job. To one who didn't know, it must have looked like I was right back where I started. But I had Jesus Christ in my life, and that was more valuable than anything I had even dreamed of having before. I knew that God's hand was on me, and I could sense that He had better things lying ahead.

CHAPTER 8

NOBODY PROMISED it would be easy, and it wasn't.

One of my brothers-in-law was in the carpet business, and he helped me get a job as a carpet installer soon after my marriage. There was nothing complicated about it; it was just plain hard work. Along with another worker, we'd pick up big rolls of carpet at the warehouse, haul them to the customer's residence, and tack the stuff down onto the floor. The pay was $60 a week, and if there is a less glamorous job somewhere, I don't know what it is.

I had almost forgotten what it was like to work for a living. I had been making $400 to $800 a week for doing what I liked most in life—singing to an audience. Now I was rolling out of bed early every morning and working hard all day for sixty lousy bucks a week.

During my work with the Birdwatchers, I had been a minor league celebrity in the South Florida area. Our group had performed fifty or sixty times on local TV stations during the past two years, and our three national TV appearances had gotten lots of local publicity. *Wild Re-*

bels had played for long engagements in the Miami-area theatres. Only a few months earlier, our full-length, bigger-than-life-size pictures had been plastered all over the city in a massive billboard campaign that gave us exposure of huge proportions.

All that was great at the time, but all it did for me now was make my job miserable. Too many people knew me. Here I was, see, in these scruffy-looking work clothes, sweating and straining to lift a ton of carpet off the truck, and some inquisitive teen-ager would peer up at me and ask, "Gee, I must be mistaken, but aren't you. . . ." and there I'd be, with nothing to do but grunt "yeah" and keep straining on the carpet.

Adults recognized me occasionally, but mainly it was the teen-agers, particularly the girls, the ones who buy all the records and go to all the dances and watch all the rock music shows on television. When one made the discovery, she usually felt compelled to tell every bobby-soxer on the block.

I suppose if you were a tenth-grade teeny-bopper it must have been a great line to lay on your fifteen-year-old friends: "Hey, wow, you won't believe this, but guess who's laying carpet over at *my* house!"

At first the whole business was embarrassing and unpleasant for me, and I got to where I wanted to wear dark glasses and a false beard whenever we went to a house where there were teen-agers. If I ignored the question, I felt rude and unfriendly. If I tried to explain, there was never time to tell the whole story, and I was afraid of sounding like a self-righteous Holy Joe. I was a carpet installer, not a preacher, for heaven's sake!

Eventually I became less self-conscious about my new identification as a Christian, and took better and better advantage of such incidents to witness about God's love in my life. The best defense is a good offense, they say, and I soon learned that the easiest way to handle potential embarrassment was to be as bold about my Christian experience as I had been in earlier days about less respectable things. I developed a rule: refuse to be intimidated. And, to my surprise, talking to people about God was much easier than trying to concoct clever ways of avoiding the subject.

Any way you look at it, laying carpet was no fun. I felt very strongly that God could use me in a more special way than that. Somehow it just didn't make sense that He would save me so marvelously, then leave me laying carpet for the rest of my life. After all, I could still sing. Maybe whatever it was about my music that turned the kids on in the secular market could be used to turn them on to Christ. So I began to pray for a chance to sing religious music.

My first opportunity came soon. It wasn't much, but it was a beginning, and I grabbed at it without hesitating. The pastor of a small church in Hollywood, Florida, heard of my conversion and invited me to come and sing for his Sunday services one week. Putting together a program was no problem; I had practically cut my teeth on an old red-backed hymnal, and the songs of the church were part of me from the bones out.

I was scared stiff that Sunday. I thought, *man, this is really stupid, getting uptight for a handful of people like this.* I had sung for thousands without a hint of nervousness before, but somehow being in church made it all different. My paralyzing fear was that they would not accept me, would not believe me when I told them that I had changed. I had thought of myself as an outsider and a misfit for so long that it was hard to believe that the church people would accept me at face value in the open, generous way they did.

As I recall, I didn't say a word through the entire service. I sang my songs and let it go at that. I figured I would leave the talking to someone else; if I could just make it through the music without choking, I would be satisfied with that.

Except for that very unimpressive attempt at religious singing, and two or three others like it, I was just a musical has-been. And a carpet layer. I seemed to be going nowhere, and things were getting pretty bleak. I got discouraged, despondent, and began to feel sorry for myself.

I was driving along in my dad's pick-up truck one day, complaining to God about how badly He was treating me, reminding Him how talented I was, and how much I wanted to use my voice for Him. *Listen, God, I'm getting tired of waiting.* I almost said it audibly, I hurled the thought so strongly at God. The answer came right back, straight from the mind of God, and it hit me with such force that it startled me. "Don't forget, Sammy, how long I waited for you." I squirmed and swallowed and felt sorry for myself no more.

Soon afterward, things began to look up. For starters, I got a new job, working as a carpenter on a local construction crew. It was better pay and the work more enjoyable.

But the real blessing came disguised as a burden, and it provided the miracle that God knew was necessary to dissolve the doubt and skepticism that still plagued Jackie.

While I was still in rock music I had developed a growth on my left eyeball, something like a cataract, but less serious. The growth got steadily larger and worse, so that it was constantly painful, and threatened to grow across the pupil of the eye, causing permanent blindness. My doctor warned that if I waited longer it might become inoperable, so I went into Holy Cross Hospital to have it removed.

The operation was a tedious, painful one, but the doctor assured me that within ten days I would be back on the job and feeling fine. Two weeks passed, three, then four weeks, and the eye was no better. After five weeks the eye was red and blood-clotted, getting worse daily, and the doctor said that the growth had come back. He told me that another operation was necessary, and set up the schedule for the next Monday. I wanted desperately not to go through the whole thing again, but my eye was excruciatingly painful, and so hideous-looking that I could hardly stand to see it in the mirror. I knew that I had to do what the doctor said.

Unless God healed me. We went to church on Sunday night and I asked the people to gather around me and pray for God to heal my eye. They prayed long and fervently, and implored God to do the work. When Jackie and I went home that night, there was no apparent change in the condition of the eye.

The next morning I got up, stumbled sleepily into the

bathroom to wash my face, and when I looked into the mirror, my left eye was clear and bright, without a sign of the growth, or a trace of the infection. It was that sudden, that simple, that direct.

I didn't know whether to shout or cry, so I just stood in front of the mirror with my mouth hanging open. The doctor could hardly believe what had happened. I never had to have the operation, and to this day my eye is as clear and unblemished as on the day I was born. It was a miracle of God as surely as there's a blue sky overhead.

Part of the miracle was its timing. For me it came when I most needed to know that God was still with me, still keeping His hand on my affairs. Just when I was tempted to believe that God had stuck me off into a corner and forgotten me, He directly intervened in this way.

For Jackie, the healing had even greater impact. The whole concept of a personal God who reaches out to people and touches them with His power was new to her, and this was visible, undeniable evidence of such a God. It was just the kind of evidence that was necessary to overcome her doubts, and make it possible for her to accept Christ as her own Lord. It was an incident which she could not lightly dismiss, and she still remembers it as the thing which brought her to God.

It wasn't easy for Jackie. When I broke with my old life, it was a simple matter of returning to what I had been taught all my life. The doctrines of salvation and healing, the informal, enthusiastic worship style, the restrictive code of Christian conduct—all of it was foreign to her. The sudden introduction that she got was a kind of shock treatment. The first worship service she attended with me after my conversion upset her so badly that she ran from the church in tears, protesting that she couldn't understand the evangelical fervor of the service inside.

With the healing of my eye, the last resistance melted. A few nights later she knelt in the altar of a little church in Pompano Beach where I was singing, and there she met Jesus Christ for herself. It was the answer to a thousand prayers, and with it our life together gained a whole new dimension of meaning and beauty. Jackie continued to grow in the faith, and it has been remarkable how the Lord has helped both of us to mature spiritually.

After that the doors seemed to open. What had been an occasional invitation to sing in churches here and there became a steady stream of requests. The word spread in the Miami area, and I began to sing all around South Florida.

As my work in the churches increased, I became more and more aware of the limitations of traditional hymns in communicating with young people. Don't get me wrong, I love the old-fashioned music of the church, and always have. Some of the best devotional experiences of my life have come from playing and singing the old church hymns.

But when it comes to the communication of the simple gospel message to teen-agers, it makes sense to unbend a little and sing songs that use their words and their kind of music. I believe that many songs which are called gospel-folk or gospel-rock can be used very effectively to win people to Christ, more effectively in some instances than the hymns and anthems we are accustomed to hearing on Sunday morning.

There has been lots of debate in the last few years over this aspect of church music. Some congregations feel that the use of electric guitars, drums, and combo organ in the sanctuary is not acceptable. Some people think it inappropriate to adapt the rock sound—its beat, its rhythms, its style of expression—to the music of the church. And I imagine many an argument has been triggered between Christian teen-agers and their parents on this very point.

When I began accepting invitations to sing in churches, I had to settle this question for myself. I don't guess there was ever any doubt about which side of the fence I would end up on. I strongly believe in the value of rock and folk forms in the work of the church, and my experiences since I made that decision have strongly reinforced it. I have seen God move miraculously in the hearts of young people through this kind of music, and I myself have worshiped through it hundreds of times.

The country-rock-folk style is not something I picked up off the shelf in the supermarket. It is *my* style. It expresses *my* feelings. When I am happy or sad, excited or blue, and I open my mouth to sing, what pours out has that folk-rock sound, and that's just the way it is. That's just *me*. And I'm sure that the same is true of thousands of Christian teen-agers. People will simply have to learn to accept that, I suppose, and realize that it is what we are saying that really matters.

The desire to express my faith in my own musical style caused me some problems in the early going, because there wasn't much of that kind of music available. I prayed for the Lord to inspire me to write new songs, songs that would let me express myself in a way that would make an impact on the kids who heard me. I didn't want them to dismiss me merely as another gospel singer; I wanted to hit them right between the eyes with my message, and jar them into doing something about it.

As He always has, God answered the prayer. I began to write Christian songs left and right. Some of them weren't so hot; but most came as I prayed for inspiration, and I have marveled at their effectiveness in reaching young people for God. The song that I still use as a theme song for all my crusades, "Turned On to Christ," was one of these. I was sitting at home alone during those early carpentering days in Fort Lauderdale, thinking about how Christ had turned me off to the old life when I surrendered to Him.

If I just knew how to tell kids that, I thought. *If I were just a better talker, and knew the words to tell them how I feel!* The urgency of that desire ate at me, and I went into the bedroom and dropped on my knees at the bed. In ten minutes the song had come. Lyrics, melody, everything. I wrote it down, and it has been my theme ever since.

Not long afterward, I was working on the fourteenth floor of a high-rise apartment building under construction in Fort Lauderdale. We were doing form work, pouring concrete into wooden forms, then tearing the forms off when the concrete hardened. It was late afternoon, and God's presence was unusually real to me. I was so preoccupied with the greatness of God, looking out over the landscape toward the horizon, that I could hardly keep my mind on my work. Which is not a very good idea when you're on the fourteenth floor.

Suddenly a line came to me, then another, and I was getting these great lyrics. It was like they were just dropping into my head. I dumped what I was doing and grabbed a two-by-four off the stack of wooden planks that lay nearby. God laid the lyrics on me and I scribbled them off on that board as fast as I could write. It was soon quitting time, so I sneaked the two-by-four out of the construction site, threw it on the front seat of my car, and headed home.

As I drove, I held that plank up with my free hand and read the lyrics over and over. I came up with a tune, and put the two together. I was singing at a midweek church service that night in Cocoa Beach, and I sang the song, "Great Big God" in that service. The next day I took the two-by-four back to the job, but I'm still using the song.

I had just finished singing at a church in Pompano Beach one night when an elderly lady came through the crowd to where I was standing. Apologetically, she pushed into my hand a church bulletin, its margins filled with scrawled handwriting. "I wrote these words while you were singing," she said self-consciously, "and I hope maybe you can do something with them."

On the way home, I turned the light on inside the automobile, and read the lyrics she had jotted down. I have no idea who that lady was, but I believe she was in tune with the Lord, because what she wrote that night became one of my best songs, "Needy People," which is still a staple of my repertoire in teen crusades. Apparently someone forgot to tell her about the generation gap, because being a gray-haired little old lady didn't slow her down a bit.

As my work before church audiences became better known, I was urged to tell the story of my conversion, and of the misery of the life which had preceded it. The first time the suggestion was made, I rejected the idea flatly. Not for me, I said. I love to sing for the Lord, but I'm not interested in exposing my past to thousands of people. Leave the preaching to the preachers, I figured. But the pastors persisted in asking that I give my testimony, especially when I was appearing before youth groups, and I began to relent.

I have always been withdrawn and introverted when it comes to my personal life. I keep things inside me even when I shouldn't sometimes; I just don't like to spill myself out to other people very much. Many of the things about my past life are embarrassing for me to tell, and I like to talk about it as little as possible. I became convinced, however, that my story could help other people; and, if it could, I had a responsibility to share it. So I gave the testimony of what God had done for me one Sunday night, with fear and trembling.

There would be many times when that testimony would help me reach people for God, but I didn't know that then. An incident occurred soon after I told my story for the first time that opened my eyes to its potential as a tool in God's hands. A young fellow named Dave went to church with his parents and heard my testimony in Fort Lauderdale. He was a glue sniffer. A few days later he had a big fight with his girlfriend, and became despondent and suicidal. He hid away from home, stuck his head in a sack of glue and inhaled for two straight days, then drank half a can of cleaning fluid.

His parents, remembering my story, called me and asked if I would go to see him in Broward General Hospital. His liver was seriously damaged, and the hospital listed his condition as critical. When I entered the room, he lay in bed with tubes in both nostrils, fluid being pumped continuously through his body. He was awake and coherent, but very weak. His bed was cluttered with those male-market sex magazines. He listened carefully while I told him all I knew about God's saving grace and healing power.

I prayed with him, and when I left I gave him my Bible for his promise to unload the magazines and read it instead. God touched him that day, and two weeks later I heard from him. He was almost fully recovered physically, and a big change had occurred in his life spiritually. *Okay, God,* I thought, *I get the point. I'll tell my story anytime there is an audience that will listen to it.*

I worked that construction job for a year, and by the end of that time was singing and giving my testimony somewhere every week. Both my older sisters are talented singers, and they had moved with their husbands to Fort Lauderdale soon after my conversion. It made a natural team: me singing and playing guitar, Bernice and Vonceil backing me up, and Don Torres (Bernice's husband) playing the piano. We worked hard. All of us had regular jobs, but we traveled and sang in South Florida constantly, at night and on weekends. We became known as the Sammy Hall Singers, and had more invitations to sing than we could accept.

Trying to work all day and sing at night was physically·draining, and the double duty began to keep us constantly exhausted. Eventually the time came to make a choice: either curtail the singing ministry or dare to step out into it full time. The latter had a second advantage: requests were now coming from other parts of the country, and we knew we could never meet any of them and continue to live in South Florida. The prospect of a full-time commitment to the Lord's work was frightening to me. I had a brand-new son (Monte, born in March of 1969), a secure job, and no promise of anything if I went on the road for God.

We were at an important crossroad, and God showed us the direction to take. In June of 1969, we drove to central Florida to sing at an old-fashioned outdoor camp meeting being held near Tampa. Thousands of people were there, and we were to sing once, at the Thursday afternoon service. When we sang, there was a spontaneous move toward the altar by dozens of teen-agers in the audience.

We were asked to stay and do a repeat that night, then the next night and the next. Four times we sang, and each time God moved in a great way. By the time the week was over, literally hundreds of kids had come to pray in the altars, and we had received scores of requests to sing in churches all over the Southeast. On the way home, we talked it over, and prayed, and talked, and prayed.

Do it now, the Lord seemed to be saying. So we did. Each of us resigned from his job on Monday. We put our houses up for sale the next day, and by the time our two-week notices had been worked out on our jobs, every house was sold. Just like that, we were on our own hook. We looked over the concert requests which we had in hand, selected Charlotte, North Carolina, as the most central base of operation, and moved there before the end of July.

Once again, God had opened the doors. All we had to do was walk through.

CHAPTER 9

SINCE I MADE THAT MOVE, God has shown me in a thousand ways that it was the right thing to do.

The first opportunity we had for a full-blown teen crusade was in Anniston, Alabama. We were scheduled for a three-night stint at the city auditorium, and all the churches in town were working hard to get ready for the occasion.

I sang at three high schools on Monday, and by the time I walked onstage for the first evening service, the auditorium was full. Each night a crowd of twelve hundred crammed the place, people standing along the walls and on the outside of the building. Each night the altars were flooded with young seekers. Each night I was more convinced than ever that I was doing what God wanted me to do.

Among the eight hundred teen-agers who found God that week were some whom I'll never forget. On the second night, six kids filed down the aisle at the invitation, all with exaggerated hippie-style clothes and appearance.

After the service was over, they came to my dressing room to rap with me. Three were dropping acid (LSD), two were shooting heroin, all were thoroughly hooked on the drug scene. I told them my story, told them they could all kick their habits if they wanted to, that God would help them stay off the junk.

I asked if they wanted to turn on to Christ, and they said yes. So they prayed, and a humbler, more sincere prayer was never prayed by any deacon in any church. They wept, thanked God for His presence, and accepted their salvation.

The last night of the crusade, two high-school boys came into the auditorium who seemed particularly important to me. They reminded me so much of myself in high school. One wore a cowboy hat; both swaggered with that self-conscious bravado that I remembered so well. At the altar an hour later, they told me their problem: booze, and too much of it. They wanted help.

As I knelt with them that night, a thought wouldn't leave me, *There you are, Sammy, just a few years ago.* I knew their story and I rejoiced with a little extra vigor when they finally prayed for Christ to deliver them. After the service they asked me to go with them to a drive-in hamburger place to get something to eat. As we sat in the car and rehashed what had happened that night, their enthusiasm was too much for them to hold down. They both got out of the car and started witnessing to their friends right there on the parking lot. It was a long time before I finally got back to the motel that night.

Those boys got close to me, and as I left Anniston the

next day the thought came again and again. *If there are that many empty, frustrated kids in Anniston, Alabama, how many millions must there be all over this country!* I could see myself in every one of them, and the desire to reach them was so strong it was almost a physical pain.

Soon after the Anniston crusade, we got our first chance to reach into one of the big cities of the North. Baltimore was to be the target for a three-day meeting, and I must admit that I was plenty uptight about the whole deal.

It was one thing to work in Anniston, and Clover, and Mount Airy, and little towns in the South. But Baltimore was different. I knew the crowds would accept me in those places, but in Baltimore there would be lots of blacks, lots of Jews, lots of Catholics, and I wasn't sure that they would even listen to me sing.

When I'm nervous I get sick, and that's what happened. The first day in Baltimore it was chilly and damp and the rain was falling in one of those drizzly, gloomy mists. I sang at four high schools that day, and the longer we went, the better I felt. At each school the kids were listening, some of them unruly at first, but always settling down and listening carefully as we got into our program. At the last two schools we worked, one predominantly black, the other mostly Jewish, the kids gave us standing ovations when we finished.

I was feeling better, but when we opened the service that night, I decided that my change of heart had been a bit premature. The audience numbered over fifteen hundred, most of them young people, including a group of about thirty or forty kids who were there to disrupt the service. They wasted no time going about their business.

They jumped over seats in the back of the auditorium, yelled loud obscenities, heckled whoever happened to be speaking from the stage between songs.

I stopped after one tune and asked them to please be quiet enough to let the audience hear, but that didn't even slow them down. As the program continued, the rest of the audience was getting more uneasy and restless, and it seemed like the whole service was about to fall apart.

The last song I was to sing before the invitation song was "Bridge Over Troubled Waters," a special, Christian version which I do of the popular Simon and Garfunkel tune. As Don Torres started the piano intro to the tune, I whispered urgently to God for help. *Do something, Lord, or this whole thing is going down the drain*, I prayed.

I began to sing, and the mood of the service changed so suddenly it was almost spooky. Everything got hushed, quiet, the kids in the back leaning forward in their seats, not saying a word. The Holy Spirit was working and the Lord's presence was so real we could almost see it, almost feel it tangibly there on the stage.

We went immediately into the invitation song, and I walked down off the stage and through the crowd as I sang. In the faces of the kids in the back I could see tears filling their eyes and creeping down their cheeks, and then there were more tears as I walked back to the stage and now they were hot and they were mine and I could not stop them.

The response to the altar appeal was led by the same

kids who had come to disrupt the service. I had never seen such a thrilling altar service before in my life, never seen such a sudden, urgent move of God's spirit. Four hundred came that night, and one thousand came before the crusade was over two nights later.

Since that week in Baltimore we have talked to literally hundreds of teen-agers—junkies, homosexuals, kids involved in sex and alcohol so deeply that they never expected to find their way out. And, over and over again, we have seen God enter their lives and change things.

I am on the road now, traveling all across the country, singing simple songs about God and telling people of how they can meet Him for themselves. I appear in schools, churches, gospel concerts, anywhere the Lord opens the door for us to go.

On the last night of a crusade at a big Baptist church in Oak Ridge, Tennessee, four guys got up from their seats during the invitation and went straight out the back door. An hour later we were breaking down our sound equipment, getting ready to leave, when the four boys burst through the door of the nearly empty sanctuary and made a beeline for me.

They poured out their story. "We had a funny feeling when you asked people to come to the altar. We wanted to go, but we didn't want to go. So we left. The farther we drove, the more miserable we felt, and we decided to come back and give it a try." They looked around at the empty church. "Is it too late?" Indeed it wasn't, and they accepted Christ then and there. We went back to Oak Ridge months later, and there were two of the four, sitting on the front row, each with a grin on his face that stretched from one sideburn to the other.

When I remember early crusades, I always think of Marietta, Georgia, a suburb of Atlanta. We've been there twice, and every time I drive through that city I think of Joe and Jim.

Joe had been an acidhead (LSD user) for four years. He came to the service one night at the Wills High School gym, and sat crosslegged on the gym floor, right in the front row. I was singing a simple gospel tune called "He Did It All for Me," when it seemed like the mood of the service just broke, and kids began to cry and accept God right in their seats. As I looked over toward where Joe was sitting, he suddenly threw both hands into the air, his face awash with tears, and prayed for salvation.

Joe came back each night after that, always bringing friends with him to seek God. When I returned to Marietta for a second meeting three months later, he came around to assure me that he was still "hanging tough," as he put it, with his new experience.

In that second crusade, an older teen-ager waited until the Marietta High School gym had almost cleared out, then came up to me to talk. His name was Jim, and he wore faded jeans, an army jacket, and an old crushed hat. "I don't believe what you're saying," he began. I paused, didn't speak, so he went on. "I don't believe people can meet Christ like you say they can."

"You can't know unless you try it," I answered him.

"That's no good," Jim replied. "If it didn't work I'd just be let down and feel worse than ever."

I urged him to meet me later in the week, when we could talk at greater length. He said maybe. As I left the gym floor and walked up through the bleachers toward the exit, a man stopped me and asked if I knew whom I had been talking with. "A kid named Jim," I answered. "A pusher named Jim," the man corrected me, and told me that Jim was one of the biggest pushers in Cobb County, that he had been in jail twice on drug charges, that he was facing a third conviction presently, and that it was impossible for anyone in the community to reach him.

I was staying that week at the home of Grover Cannon, a Marietta layman whose family had become close friends of mine. Jim came by their house to see me the next day, and we talked. Rick Evatt, a Georgia Tech football player who works with the teens at a Marietta church, was with us, and all day long we rapped with Jim about his need for God. That night, the last of the crusade, he was in the service again, and the whole night I thought about him as we worked.

When I gave the altar invitation, kids came by the scores down the aisles, but I wasn't satisfied. Jim was on my mind and I urgently wanted God to touch him. My attention was diverted for a moment by something off to my left, and as I looked off in that direction, something hit me like a body block on the right.

It was Jim. He threw his arms around my neck and shouted into my ear, "God has touched me! God has saved me!" And so God had! The next night was a special follow-up service at the Roswell Street Baptist Church. Not only was Jim there, but he brought a carload of friends with him, and led them to Christ before the service was over.

I wouldn't want anyone to get the idea that God's grace works only for teen-agers. Not on your life! I could tell you about God helping adults as well—a truck driver who was hooked on bennies, a housewife in her early thirties who had become a near alcoholic, a grandmother who had become depressed and suicidal at the death of her husband.

A forty-five-year-old lady called me late one night in Charlotte. She had read my story in a newspaper article, and called me in desperation. She had suffered severe migraine headaches, and had used frequent morphine injections to control the pain. Now the headaches were no problem, but she was hopelessly addicted to morphine, and the doctor had told her she would never get off.

She was on three fixes a day; she had periods when she couldn't control herself, and would beat her teen-age daughter and scream at her husband. Her family was at the breaking point and so was she. She drove to Charlotte, and became convinced that Christ was the answer to her problems. When she prayed, God touched her. Several months later we were still hearing from her, testifying that she had kicked morphine for good that night, that God had completely reversed her life, and that she was still living for Him.

When I left the Birdwatchers, I told my old friends goodbye, and never expected to see them again. It is almost uncanny how many of them have crossed my path since that time.

One of the groupies who spent a lot of time at one of the nightclubs when I was with the Birdwatchers was a girl named Sandy Simonds. She was a fairly typical groupie, and had a special in with Jimi Hendrix, the famous rock musician who died of a drug overdose a few years ago.

Sandy was well-liked around the club, where everyone knew her, and knew that she was an out-and-out junkie. She came from an upper-middle-class family, but had gone into hard drugs with a vengeance. When I knew her last she was shooting heroin into her veins to the tune of sixty dollars a day, and when I left the Birdwatchers, I never expected to see her again.

Not long ago I was visiting Surfside Challenge, a Christian coffeehouse ministry in Miami directed by the Reverend Tommy Morse. I was in the lobby of the mission, saw someone start down the staircase from upstairs, and couldn't believe my eyes. *I must be out of my mind*, I thought. There was nothing to do but ask.

"Sandy, is that you?" I asked weakly. The answer came back bright and cheerful. "You bet your life it is! How're you doing, Sammy?"

It was Sandy Simonds. She told me the story of how she had gone to the Dade County Jail to see a friend and had heard of the Christian mission there in Miami. When her fortunes reached rock bottom, she went to Surfside Challenge and agreed to go cold turkey to kick the heroin habit. God saved her there on the spot, helped her get off the drug, and made a spectacular change in her life. She is now on the staff at the mission in Miami, and is helping other addicts find help through the work of the Holy Spirit.

Another nightclub patron whom I had known well in the Birdwatcher days I met recently in other, less pleasant circumstances. He had been a pusher in Miami, always wheeling and dealing with every drug you could name, and I had bought from him often in the early days.

I sang at the Florida State Penitentiary, several months ago, and stayed awhile to talk to some of the inmates after the service. Up walked my friend the pusher, wearing the crude cotton shirt and plain grey trousers of the prison uniform. He asked if I remembered him, and told me about the armed robbery that had resulted in the fifty-five- and thirty-two-year sentences he was serving. I tried to witness to him, but he was not interested.

There have been numerous occasions when I have met friends from my former life and had the opportunity to tell them about my conversion. I was able to lead one of them to the Lord, and I suppose his experience meant more to me than anyone else who has been saved in my services. His name was Gary Smith, and he is my cousin.

Gary was too young to drink legally while I was in rock music, so I bought his drinks for him, and enjoyed showing him what a swinging, big-shot cousin he had. By the time I was converted, he was already well on the way to serious drug abuse, and my experience came too late to have much of an impact on him.

One day in Charlotte I got a phone call from my aunt in Fort Myers. She told me that Gary had gotten a batch of bad LSD, and had freaked out wildly in a dangerous chemical overdose. The experience had sobered him, and now that he was well enough to travel, he wanted to come to Charlotte to talk with me. When I met him at the airport the next day, I couldn't believe it was Gary. He was drawn and pale, his skin stretched tightly over the bones from loss of weight, and was only a shadow of the healthy, robust Gary I had known before.

I was singing that night in Charlotte, and Gary went with me. All the way there he asked questions about the Christian life, and I answered the best I could. I sang every song that night with a silent prayer for Gary, and when the altar call was given, he came forward to give his life to Christ. He stayed with me a few weeks before returning to Florida, and not long afterward followed God's call into the coffeehouse ministry, joining my brother Jimmy to open a place called "The Seed" in Knoxville, Tennessee. The two of them and their wives are there now, ministering daily to runaways, winos, hippies, and students at the University of Tennessee.

Life doesn't begin and end on the stage. As great as His blessing in my work has been, His presence in my private life has been just as real.

One of the first things that I learned as a Christian was that I still had to get up in the morning and put my pants on one leg at a time just like always. Being a Christian, even being in a full-time Christian ministry, didn't exempt me from the daily pressures and problems of life that everyone must face.

Again and again God has met my needs. Once Jackie

and I went camping in the Smoky Mountains, taking our son Monte, then a year old. Monte became sick and we headed back to Charlotte. As we drove, late in the afternoon, his condition grew steadily worse, his vomiting more frequent, and by the time we got home, his temperature climbed to 106 degrees.

When we put him to bed that night, Jackie and I slept on the floor in his bedroom to be close to him during his restless, feverish sleep. At about 3:00 A.M., Monte went into convulsions, and we were badly scared. I picked him up out of his bed, and carried him to the bathroom to try to bring his fever down by putting him in cold water. He unaccountably stopped breathing, and by the time I had filled the tub, he was turning blue. It seemed like the life had gone out of him.

Jackie was crying, almost hysterically. I didn't know what was wrong with him, didn't know what to do. I prayed. I asked God to heal him, to please heal him and bring him around. When I looked down, Monte opened his eyes and started to breathe again. The fever broke, there were no more convulsions, and within minutes his temperature was normal. We took him to the hospital just to make sure, and before we even got there the sickness was gone. I'm not a doctor, and I don't know much about medicine, but I know what happened that night. God healed my son, and He did it in a way that strengthened my faith and love for Him.

The Holy Spirit helps me daily in less dramatic ways. I am learning to go to Him when I'm confused, or blue, or discouraged. A few months after I moved to North

Carolina, I was badly in need of guidance. I was being advised to do this and do that, getting all kinds of conflicting opinions. I knew what I felt God wanted me to do, but it didn't agree with all the advice I was getting, and I didn't know which move to make.

Near dark one night, I went out to a little lake near Charlotte with my Bible and sat on the pier asking the Lord to help me.

My Bible fell open to 1 John 2, and my eye came to rest on verse 27: "But the anointing which ye have received of him abideth in you, and ye need not that any man teach you: but as the same anointing teacheth you . . . ye shall abide in him." That was my answer. I embraced it and walked home knowing exactly which direction God wanted me to take.

Twice I have had flashbacks. These are terrifying experiences which all former LSD users fear so much, when for no apparent reason the symptoms of some former drug trip suddenly reoccur. Both times I have been lying in bed early in the morning, just awake, enjoying the last few moments before getting up, when the flashback occurred.

My mind started to rush, that panicky, sickening feeling that I had felt in earlier days on drugs. I slid off the bed onto my knees, frightened by my own helplessness. I had enough presence of mind to pray, *Lord, take it away, don't let it happen, I'm your child.* And, both times, it stopped just that suddenly, leaving me shaken and breathless, but more aware than ever of the reality of God's resources in my life.

Some people think that because God delivered me from sin once in my life, I never have to worry about it again. That just isn't true. Occasionally I get to thinking about those drug experiences I had which were pleasant, and I feel the temptation to turn on again. I simply have to say no, to ignore the desire and pray for God to help me over it.

The flashbacks have certainly helped in that regard. They have reminded me of the other side of the coin, and kept me from the easy mistake of forgetting the bad and remembering only the good. The real desire for the old life is gone; God has taken it away. But still there are times that temptation comes creeping in, and I just have to be honest about it and resist it when it comes.

I have a lot to learn about living for God, but I think I've already learned the most important thing: that, wherever I am, whatever my situation, Jesus Christ is there to live His life through me. I've learned that I can depend on that twenty-four hours a day, every day of my life. And that, I believe, is half the battle.

CHAPTER 10

"Hey, what's your kick, man?"

I was standing backstage in the auditorium in Birmingham, Alabama, when he stepped up to me, poked his face almost into mine, and asked the question.

His hair was long, long, long, and his clothes looked like something off a rummage-sale rack after all the good stuff had been taken. He was a cast member of the rock opera *Hair*, and his traveling troupe was pulling into the auditorium as mine was pulling out. He had heard me sing and speak and he had a question to ask.

"Hey, what's your kick, man?" It was a challenge but it was an honest question, too, and I got the feeling he really was puzzled. "Why do you knock the good time scene so hard, man, telling these kids to lay off drugs and liquor and all that good stuff? Why push the Jesus bit to these kids when they are just now old enough to have a good time? What's the big rush, man?"

Good question. And one that I hear hundreds of times a year, everywhere I go, from teen-agers of every possible

117

description. "Why the Jesus bit *now?* Why when we're young? Why say no to sex and drugs and booze tonight— why not wait until we're full-fledged adults before we go straight?"

Believe it or not, I like to hear that question. No matter how many times I get it from fresh, open-faced fifteen-year-old girls, or bearded, scruffy-looking longhairs, or clean-cut, Boy Scout types, I like to hear the question. Why? Because it's a good question, and I think I've got a good answer.

"Why now?" they ask, and I could take all night to answer. I could tell about a boy named Mike, in Statesville, North Carolina, who was the student body president at the high school where we did a concert. He met us that afternoon, told us who he was, and got the information he needed to make the introduction to the audience.

A good-looking guy, Mike. Tall and fair, with sandy blonde hair, he was smooth and friendly, and it wasn't hard to see why he was such a popular guy at the high school. After we sang that day, I gave an altar invitation, and Mike walked down the long aisle, tears pouring down his face, with all eyes turned his way.

Mike prayed the benediction that day, and said good-bye to us warmly as we left the school. We got a letter three weeks later saying that Mike had testified to his conversion practically every day after we left—and that he had been killed two weeks later, drowned with two of his buddies while swimming in a pond.

"Why meet Christ now?" they ask, and I tell them about Mike. Or about another boy in Sparta, North Carolina, the same spring, who accepted Christ in one of our one-night stands at his high school, and was killed that weekend in an automobile accident.

"Why now?" It's a good question, and I don't have to talk about death to answer it. I could answer it by reading letters I get, letters that tell of habits grown hard-to-break because they've been allowed to go so far. Listen to this one:

> You may not remember who I am, but you met me here in Canton (Ohio), and you asked me to stop my smoking pot. Well, I kept my promise about *trying* to stop, but it is so hard to stop. I am trying so hard; I guess maybe not hard enough. Please pray with me that I may receive the will-power to overcome this habit.
>
> Sammy, I want to become a Christian so much: please help pray with me before I go too far and won't want help.

"Why now?" I don't have to talk about drugs to answer that question. I could answer it by pointing to lives soiled and saddened by guilt. I could answer it with a letter from a girl in New Jersey, who told me her story because she had to tell it to someone:

> If I'm going to have any peace at all then I'll tell you the whole story from the beginning to the end. It all started when I was fifteen and determined to go with this guy that is about six

years older than I am. We went to a movie that I shouldn't have seen in the first place. Well, about halfway through the movie we decided to go somewhere that we could be alone. He kissed me and the next thing I knew we were in the back seat of his car. I went all the way and this has been going on for four years, not every weekend, just about two to three times a month. I've let him talk me into staying out of school so we could go to motels to have our fun . . . I sat there and listened to you tell what had happened to you before you became a Christian. I said if Sammy Hall can do it so can I.

Sammy, you're the first person I've ever told the whole story to. I've tried before but I just couldn't go on because something inside me wouldn't let me tell everything. Now that I've told you please help me to find myself and get back to God. I was too stubborn to listen to what was right.

Part of the sad truth about sin is that it leaves its mark, even when the sinning is over. Some kids think they can break God's laws over and over, then ask for forgiveness and all the trouble sin causes goes away. That is simply not true. God forgives, and gives new life, but sin still leaves its mark, and sometimes it is a painful one.

The smart kid is the one who meets God *now*, who doesn't wait, doesn't mess around with things that can destroy him, not even for a week or a day. Why accept

Christ now? I could tell you how sin can get its hook in
your jaw, and make life a battle even when you want to
go straight. Here's a letter from a guy in Florida:

> I manage to stay pretty prayed up and I go
> to church every chance I get, but there is one
> thing that is a real problem. I think even you
> would be surprised to find out how easy it is to
> get grass, and this may sound stupid, but al-
> though I go to church all the time and I pray
> —maybe not as much as I should—still when I
> have the opportunity to score a number, you
> will never believe the overpowering urge that
> says there is nothing wrong with doing one
> trick. You go to church all the time and you
> know better than to take anything stronger. I
> feel like I'll just do it this one time, and
> brother when I say I get the urge—I don't
> mean just a desire. I mean it's like everything
> transforms and I don't even think twice about
> it. And then when I'm done I'll feel terrible,
> and I'll get down and pray, dear Lord forgive
> me, give me the strength to stand up against
> this, and take the desire away.

Every time I sing, I urge young people to accept
Christ as personal Saviour, and I urge them to do it
now. Every day lived outside God's love is a mistake,
and the results of that mistake are sometimes difficult
to undo. There is only one way to overhaul a life that

Satan has ruined, and that is by a complete surrender to Jesus Christ—the sooner, the better.

"But does any of it last?"

The man who put the question to me was a preacher; there was no doubt about that. He had all the marks of an energetic busy pastor of a typical First-Baptist-Church-on-the-corner. He was articulate, well-groomed, with that good firm handshake and warm manner.

We were at a ministers' convention in Missouri, but if I had met him on the street somewhere instead, I think I would have known that he was a preacher anyway.

He had heard me speak on the need of reaching teens, ministering to drug addicts, getting the gospel to the hippies, the bikers, the potheads, all the kids of this generation. And when he asked the question, it was an honest one, but oozing with doubt and misgiving that verged on outright skepticism.

"Does any of it last? Do these kids really have a change in their lives? After they've come to the altar and prayed, what happens then? I mean, maybe your case is the exception to the rule; maybe to these kids a religious experience is just some kind of fad, and they go out the door and right back to their old problems. Does any of it last, I mean *really* last?"

That question is the one I hear more than any other in my work. Mostly from adults, I think, who are a bit skeptical about conversion stories, or who believe that "once a junkie, always a junkie" stuff. But it is asked by the kids, too, who genuinely want to know if turning to Christ can be a permanent solution to their problems.

Of course it can last! And does, for literally thousands of kids all over the country. Can it really change a life?

Ask Ken O'Brien. He walked into a crusade service in Tampa one night, so low he felt like the end had come for him. His was the classic story of the teen-age drug user: marijuana at fourteen, shooting up (injecting into the vein) morphine by age sixteen, a short stretch in the Vero Beach city jail on drug possession. He was seventeen now, and had been given one of my LP albums by a friend. So he came to hear me sing.

Ken came to me after the concert and said he had to talk. I could tell he meant business. We went down to the beach at Tampa Bay, near where I was staying, and walked and talked until early morning. At 2:30 A.M., standing there on the wet sand, we held hands and prayed and he was born again. He began immediately to witness to his friends, and a few months later began full-time youth work. I still hear from Ken often, and he is living and working for God, steady as a rock.

Does it really last? Ask one Alabama working girl, twenty-two years old, who came forward in an altar service and made a commitment. She told me this in a letter several months later:

> We had our class reunion last Saturday night and I didn't drink a thing but Coke and this shocked everybody. I had as much fun, if not more, than anyone there. The thing that thrilled me so was that I didn't want any and that I could tell the people why. I witnessed all week at work about the wonderful change that God made in

my life and several of the girls said they wished that they could change too. Help me pray for these girls.

Does it really last? Ask Ray Roberts. He grew up in Miami, his parents divorced, one brother a homosexual suicide victim, another brother serving a prison sentence for life. Ray got into drugs and crime, and did two years in the state penitentiary for robbery.

When he got out, he went to the West Coast, and there became involved in organized crime. He broke into a large university, stole thousands of dollars of laboratory equipment, and worked for the syndicate making LSD for distribution to pushers all over the country.

Somewhere along the way the mob turned on Ray, and he fled the West Coast, flew back into Miami, and hid out in Fort Lauderdale, boarding with two elderly women there. They were Christians, had no idea of Ray's background, and insisted that he go with them to a local church to hear me sing during one of my meetings there. And so he came into the church one night, nervous and jumpy as a barefoot boy on a hot tar road.

The service moved him, and he walked forward in response to the invitation. The Lord saved him. He kicked his drug usage immediately, laid low for a while longer, then went to work for Surfside Challenge, the Christian inner-city ministry in Miami. He is still a witnessing, working Christian in Miami this very day.

Can a Christian experience really deliver a life from misery? Ask an eighteen-year-old girl named Debby, who was a junkie in North Carolina, shooting heroin daily, sick of the habit and too badly hooked to get off, she thought. She called me on the phone, crying and praying for two hours late one night, and finally made a commitment to Christ that she felt was genuine and permanent.

She hung up after that and I didn't know the outcome until two months later. A girl walked up to me in a church in Mount Airy, North Carolina, and said simply, "I'm Debby, and I'm still living for God." She shoved up her sleeve and showed me an arm covered with old needle scars, the "track marks" of the heroin user. She hadn't had a fix since the night we had talked, and is now living in a small North Carolina town, working with the police to fight the drug traffic there.

Does it last? Read this spot of a letter from a guy in Nashville, Tennessee. I received it on November 22, after being in Nashville in early July. It is simple and to the point:

> I've got good news for you, Sammy. I haven't used any form of drugs since July 3rd. Well, I quit (boy, was it rough) . . . I got married three weeks ago Saturday, and we are really happy.

Can a teen-ager's experience with God really last? The answer, overwhelmingly, is yes, and it doesn't take a junkie to experience the change. Christ's presence is just as real, and just as lasting, to the average high-school student who surrenders to the Lord. Here's part of a letter from Atlanta, Georgia:

I was at your crusade on Tuesday night and since then my whole life has changed.

Do you remember those "Turn On to Christ" buttons you had at the crusade? Well, I got one and wore it to school. A lot of kids just stared, others called me a fanatic and others smiled! One boy asked me what I was trying to prove. I said that I wasn't proving anything, but that I loved the Lord. He looked at me and said you're kidding. I said no! I told him that I was proud to wear it, Sammy, what else could I have told him? I want to help so many kids!

And here is another one from a new convert who wrote from New Haven, Indiana:

God is really working in New Haven, so many kids are becoming Christians as a result of our Bible study at school. In literature class we're really getting into some great discussions on *The Screwtape Letters*. Now we're talking about witnessing and everyone is really getting on fire for Jesus! Wow, is it ever great!

Is it ever great! I guess that is the most typical expression I could quote from the newborn Christian. It conveys all the wonder and excitement and thrill of discovery that comes to those who surrender their lives, holding nothing back, to God's will for them.

EPILOGUE

I AM LIVING now in Sevier County, Tennessee, ten miles from the nearest town, on a ridge just across the valley from English Mountain. It is a quiet, country place, and I like being there on those rare times when I am not on the road.

Sometimes I sit at night on the side of the ridge outside my house, and look across at the mountain, outlined darkly by the moon. And I hear those good, outdoor sounds that you can hear only in the countryside late at night. And I think about the raucous laughter, the blinding lights, the noise and clamor of the world I left behind. And then I think about those thousands of young faces that have looked up at me with the joy of newfound life reflected in their eyes, testifying to Christ's work in their hearts.

And then I think, *My God, how far you've brought me.* What a long, long way from the misery and desperation of that unhappy, hollow life.

And then I remember how many are still out there.

How many are still empty and lonely and lost. How many are still looking for life in a pill, or a joint, or the beat of a bass guitar.

And then I feel restless again and I want to leave the quiet countryside and leave my mountain and go to where they are and tell them what God can do for them. I'm hooked on a good thing now. I'm hooked on telling the story of Christ now, hooked on the constant presence of God, on the power of His Spirit when He grabs a heart and shakes it free from sin.

I'm hooked on God's love, and as long as there are people out there who haven't heard, I'll be out there telling them that they can be hooked on a good thing too!

**Sammy Hall at
Church of God General Assembly 1972**

Sammy 1972

Sammy in 1973

Family, Atlanta Georgia 1980

Fun Downunder, Bungee in Australia (18-ft)

New Zealand Alps

Family at Pearl Harbor—Cori, Brannon, Monte

Sammy & Monte, Germany 1989

Christmas 1992

With Ronald Reagan 1992

Family Portrait, 1996

Sammy & Jackie

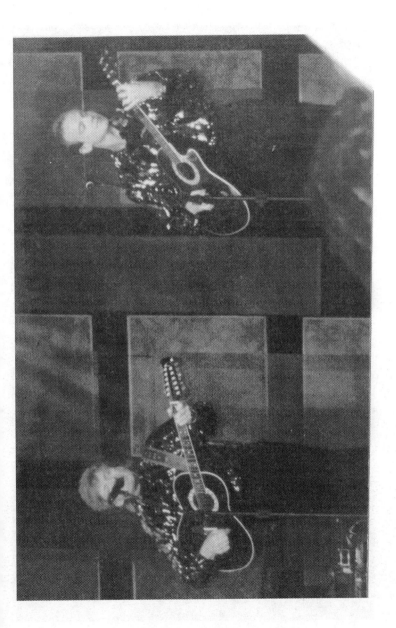

CCMA Awards Show — 2001

CCMA Awards Show with the Family
2002 Duo of the Year - Monte & Sammy

Grandson Brennen

Me and my grandson

Cori, Jackie's mother, Brennen & Jackie

Austin & Sabrina, Grandchildren